RESEARCH BIBLIOGRAPHIES & CHECKLISTS

9

Du Bellay: a bibliography

RESEARCH BIBLIOGRAPHIES & CHECKLISTS

R_CB

General editors

A. D. Deyermond, J. R. Little and J. E. Varey

DU BELLAY

a bibliography

MARGARET BRADY WELLS

Grant & Cutler Ltd
1974

I.S.B.N. 84-399-2606-5

DEPÓSITO LEGAL: V. 3.206 - 1974

Printed in Spain by Artes Gráficas Soler, S.A., Valencia

for

GRANT & CUTLER LTD
11, BUCKINGHAM STREET, LONDON, W.C.2.

CONTENTS

INTRODUCTION

The aim of this bibliography is to provide a list of critical works referring principally to Du Bellay. A list of editions of Du Bellay's works is also included, but this is confined to editions published after 1750, and no attempt has been made at a descriptive bibliography of early editions, as bibliographies of this type are already available (see section A).

The bibliography is divided as follows:

A: Editions of Du Bellay's works, after 1750.

    a: Complete works

    b: *La Deffence et Illustration de la Langue Françoyse*

    c: *L'Olive*

    d: *Divers Jeux Rustiques*

    e: *Les Regrets, Les Antiquitez de Rome, Songe*

Items are presented in chronological order.

B: Critical works relating to Du Bellay

    a: Books and theses devoted principally to Du Bellay

    b: Articles and chapters of books devoted mainly to Du Bellay

    c: Theses on sixteenth-century literature which, judging from the abstracts, when available, are likely to be of interest (*Dissertation Abstracts* and similar references are given wherever possible)

    d: Books in which significant reference is made to Du Bellay

    e: Articles and chapters of books in which significant reference is made to Du Bellay

Items are presented alphabetically by author. Two or more items by the same author are presented chronologically.

All items are numbered in sequence within each section, and cross-references are given when necessary (e.g. Bb56). Items in both main sections are followed by critical reviews (where appropriate) and these, listed alphabetically by author, are attached to the item by a decimal point.

Items in books and periodicals are presented differently:

Book item: Surname, forename or initials, chapter title in single quotation marks, book title in italics, place of publication: publisher, year of publication, page numbers. E.g. Bb14 Belloc, Hilaire, 'J. Du B.', in *Avril, being essays on the*

poetry of the French Renaissance, London: Duckworth, 1904, pp. 151–94. *Periodical item:* Surname, forename or initials, article title in single quotation marks, periodical title (generally abbreviated) in italics, volume in Roman numerals, date in parentheses with English abbreviations (e.g. 4.12.25 = 4th December 1925; Aut. 1967 = Autumn 1967), page numbers. E.g. Bb162 Merrill, Robert V., 'Du B.'s *Olive* 112 and the *Rime Diverse*', *MLN,* LX (1945), 527–30. For dates prior to 1910 the year is given in full (e.g. 15.12.1900).

A list of abbreviations of recurring periodical titles is given. The following abbreviations have also been used: Du B. = Du Bellay; J. Du B. = Joachim Du Bellay; *La Défense* = *La Deffence et Illustration de la Langue Françoyse; D.J.R. = Divers Jeux Rustiques.* An index of names, and another of references to main compositions, to the Pléiade, the sonnet, and the ode are given.

I have not been able to see all the items personally, and those not seen are marked with an asterisk. Some of these items (found in bibliographies or reviews) are, unfortunately, not always complete, and I should be grateful for any help in filling these gaps.

Certain omissions from this bibliography are deliberate. I have excluded references in general histories of French literature and in encyclopaedias. Modern critical editions of works by Du Bellay's contemporaries nearly always include references to him in their introduction – however, to have included all these critical editions would have widened the scope of this bibliography far beyond its aim, and so these, too, have been excluded. The same reason excludes many purely biographical works on sixteenth-century writers, although it has been necessary to include more general works on Du Bellay's contemporaries, especially Ronsard.

Whilst I have tried to include all material published before Easter 1973 I am aware that there will inevitably be omissions. I should be most grateful for information which will bring the bibliography nearer its aim of completeness.

My main sources of information have been the standard bibliographies and the cumulative indexes of various periodicals. Various library catalogues have also been consulted, and my task was considerably lightened by the ready help of library staff, in particular those of the Taylor Institution, Oxford. I am most grateful to friends and colleagues who have helped in a variety of ways, especially to Mr Gordon Humphreys of Leeds University for his assistance in locating theses and periodical items. I am deeply indebted to Dr Roger Little for his patient guidance and invaluable advice, and to my husband for his constant support – their encouragement has been very much appreciated.

M.B.W.

Edinburgh & Oxford, Easter 1973.

ABBREVIATIONS

AP	*Archives de Philosophie*
Archiv	*Archiv für das Studium der neueren Sprachen*
Ass. G. Budé	*Association Guillaume Budé*
AUMLA	*Journal of the Australasian Language and Literature Association*
AUP	*Annales de l'Université de Paris*
BBB	*Bulletin du bibliophile et du bibliothécaire*
BGB	*Bulletin Guillaume Budé*
BHR	*Bibliothèque d'Humanisme et de Renaissance*
BRP	*Beiträge zur romanischen Philologie*
Bull. it.	*Bulletin italien*
Bull. Soc. Cholet	*Bulletin de la Société des Sciences, Lettres et Beaux-Arts de Cholet*
Bull. Soc. Sens	*Bulletin de la Société des Sciences, Lettres et Beaux-Arts de Sens*
CAIEF	*Cahiers de l'Association Internationale des Etudes françaises*
Comp. Lit.	*Comparative Literature*
DA	*Dissertation Abstracts*
EC	*Esprit Créateur*
Et. class.	*Etudes classiques*
FM	*Le Français moderne*
FMLS	*Forum for Modern Language Studies*
FR	*French Review*
FS	*French Studies*
HR	*Humanisme et Renaissance*
Mem. Acad. Angers	*Mémoires de l'Académie des Sciences, Belles-Lettres et Arts d'Angers*
Mem. Acad. Toulouse	*Mémoires de l'Académie des Sciences, Inscriptions et Belles-Lettres de Toulouse*
Mem. Soc. Angers	*Mémoires de la Société nationale d'agriculture, sciences et arts d'Angers*
MLN	*Modern Language Notes*
MLQ	*Modern Language Quarterly*
MLR	*Modern Language Review*
MP	*Modern Philology*
NRF	*La Nouvelle Revue Française*
PMLA	*Publications of the Modern Language Association of America*

RBPH	*Revue belge de philologie et d'histoire*
RCC	*Revue des cours et conférences*
RDM	*Revue des Deux Mondes*
Ren. News	*Renaissance News*
Ren. Q.	*Renaissance Quarterly*
RF	*Revue de France*
RHLF	*Revue d'histoire littéraire de la France*
RLC	*Revue de littérature comparée*
RLR	*Revue des langues romanes*
RLV	*Revue des langues vivantes*
Rom. Jahrb.	*Romanistisches Jahrbuch*
Rom. Phil.	*Romance Philology*
Rom. Rev.	*Romanic Review*
RPFP	*Revue de philologie française et provençale*
RR	*Revue de la Renaissance*
RSH	*Revue des Sciences Humaines*
RSS	*Revue du seizième siècle*
SP	*Studies in Philology*
St. fr.	*Studi francesi*
St. Ren.	*Studies in the Renaissance*
YWMLS	*Year's Work in Modern Language Studies*
ZFSL	*Zeitschrift für französische Sprache und Literatur*
ZRP	*Zeitschrift für romanische Philologie*

EDITIONS OF DU BELLAY'S WORKS AFTER 1750
For bibliographies of early editions see Bb58, 281;
See also Bb39, 52, 128, 129, 151, 155

COMPLETE WORKS
* * *

Aa1   *Œuvres françoises* . . . avec une notice biographique et des notes par C. Marty-Laveaux, Paris: A. Lemerre, 1866, 1867.
.1 Colincamp, J., *La Presse* (1.11.1868).
.2 Roqueplan, N., Feuilleton du *Constitutionnel* (30.12.1866).
.3 See Bb226.

Aa2   *Œuvres complètes* . . . avec un commentaire historique et critique par Léon Séché, Paris: Revue de la Renaissance, 1903–13. Issued as supplements to *RR*.
.1 Vianey, J., *RHLF*, X (1903), 523–5.

Aa3   *Œuvres poétiques* . . . Edition critique publiée par Henri Chamard, Paris: Droz (S.T.F.M.), 1908–31.
.1 Plattard, J., *RSS*, I (1913), 449.
.2 Silver, I, *MLN*, LXXVIII (1963), 88–90.
.3 Sozzi, L., *St. fr.*, XVI (1962), 135; XIX (1963), 141–2.

Aa4   *Poésies françaises et latines* . . . avec notice et notes par E. Courbet, Paris: Garnier, 1918. A selection of the Latin poetry may be found in *Amœnitates poeticae,* sive Theodori Bezae, Marci-Antonii Mureti, et Joannis Secundi Juvenilia: tum Joannis-Bonefonii Pancharis: Joachimi Bellaii Amores &c. &c., Lugduni-Batavorum, Voeneunt Parisiis: Apud Josephum Barbou, 1779.*
For a French translation of the Latin verse see Ba56.

Aa5   *Poésies* . . . texte établi et annoté par Marcel Hervier. Gravures de Deusenry, Paris: Edns Richelieu, 1954–6.

LA DEFFENCE ET ILLUSTRATION DE LA LANGUE FRANÇOYSE
* * *

Ab1   *La Défense* . . . Précédée d'un Discours sur le bon usage de la langue française par Paul Ackermann, Paris: Crozet, 1839.

Ab2   *La Défense* . . . introduction et commentaire par J. Tell, Brussels: imprimerie de F. Callewaert père, 1875.*

Ab3   *La Défense* . . . avec introduction, notes . . . suivie du
        Quintil Horatien (de C. Fontaine), par Em. Person, Versailles:
        Cerf et fils, 1878, Paris: Cerf, 1887, 1892. Part of a series
        called "Bibliothèque historique de la Langue Française pub-
        liée sous la direction de A. Chassang".

Ab4   *La Défense,* Paris: Vrin, 1892.*

Ab5   *La Défense* . . . avec une notice biographique et un com-
        mentaire historique et critique par Léon Séché, Paris: Revue
        de la Renaissance, 1901; Paris: E. Sansot et Cie., 1905. A
        separate issue of pp. 1–83 of Aa2.

Ab6   *La Défense* . . . édition critique par Henri Chamard, Paris:
        Fontemoing, 1904; Paris: Didier (S.T.F.M.), 1948.
        .1 Anon., *RR,* IV (1904), 136.
        .2 England, S.L., *YWMLS,* XI (1940–9), 48.
        .3 Huguet, E., *RHLF,* XII (1905), 158–9.
        .4 Laumonier, P., *Revue critique* (10.10.1904).

Ab7   *La Défense* . . . suivie du projet de l'œuvre intitulée *De la
        précellence du langage françois,* par Henri Estienne. Nouvelle
        édition revue et annotée par Louis Humbert, Paris: Garnier,
        1914, 1930.

Ab8   *La Défense* [with 'Bibliographische Notiz' signed E.L., i.e.
        Erhard Lommatzsch], Berlin : Weidmann, 1920.*

Ab9   *La Défense,* Berlin, 1921. Romanische Texte, II.*

Ab10   *La Défense* . . . par I.D.B.A., Paris: C. Aveline, 1925.
        (Maastricht: Edns Traiectum ad Mosam).*

Ab11   *La Défense* . . . *Poésies choisies* . . . Introduction par Alphonse
        Séché, Paris: Edn Lutetia, 1936.

Ab12   *La Défense* . . . Avant-propos de Charles Braibant, Lille:
        Librairie Giard, 1949.*

Ab13   *La Défense* . . . Facsimile de l'édition originale de 1549
        publiée, . . . avec une introduction de Fernand Desonay,
        Lille, Geneva: Droz, 1950.
        .1 England, S.L., *YWMLS,* XII (1950), 29.
        .2 François, A., *RHLF,* LII (1952), 378–9.
        .3 Orr, J., *MLR,* XLVI (1951), 104–5.

Ab14   *La Défense,* ed. L. Terreaux, Paris: Bordas, 1972.
        .1 Camproux, C., *RLR,* LXXX (1972), 500–1.

        For another edition, see Ba34.
        For English translations of *La Défense* see Ba65, 68.

L'OLIVE
* * *

Ac1   *L'Olive 1550,* Paris: Société littéraire de France, 1922.
(Collection des Cent cinquante).*

DIVERS JEUX RUSTIQUES
* * *

Ad1   *D.J.R. et autres oeuvres poétiques de J. Du B., Angevin,*
Collationné sur la première édition (Paris 1558), Paris:
I. Liseux, 1875.

Ad2   *D.J.R.,* publiés sur l'édition originale de 1558 et augmentés
des lettres de l'auteur, avec une notice de Guill. Colletet,
une bibliographie et des notes par Adolphe Van Bever,
Paris: Sansot, 1912.
  .1 Gourmont, R. de, *Mercure de France,* CI (Feb. 1913),
      812–3.
  .2 Plattard, J., *RSS,* I (1913), 449.

Ad3   *D.J.R.,* édition critique publiée par Henri Chamard.
Paris: Didier (S.T.F.M.), 1947. Extract from vol.V of Aa3.

Ad4   *D.J.R.,* [Nouvelle] édition critique commentée par V. L.
Saulnier, Geneva: Droz, Lille: Giard, Paris: Minard, 1947
and 1965.
  .1 England, S.L., *YWMLS,* XI (1940–9), 44.
  .2 Jourda, P., *RHLF,* XLIX (1949), 84.
  .3 Lytton Sells, A., *FS,* III (1949), 273–4.
  .4 McFarlane, I. D., *YWMLS,* XXVIII (1966), 69.

Ad5   *D.J.R.,* Gravures originales au burin de Paul Leuguet,
Paris: Vialetay, 1961.*

LES REGRETS, LES ANTIQUITEZ DE ROME, SONGE
* * *

Ae1   *Les Regrets de J. Du B. angevin,* Collationné sur la première
édition (Paris, 1558), Paris: I. Liseux, 1876.

Ae2   *Les Regrets de J. Du B. angevin (1558),* avec une introduction,
des notes et un index par Robert de Beauplan, agrégé de
l'Université, Paris: Sansot, 1907.
  .1 Bonnefon, P., *RHLF,* XV (1908), 188–9.
  .2 Gourmont, J. de, *Mercure de France,* LXXVI (Nov. 1908),
      109.
  .3 Rouxière, J. de la, *RR,* VIII (1908), 197.

Ae3   *Antiquités de Rome, contenant une générale description de sa grandeur et comme une déploration de sa ruine: plus un songe ou vision sur le même sujet.* Frontispice gravé sur bois par Jacques Beltrand, Paris: Société littéraire de France, 1919.*

Ae4   *Les Regrets de J. Du B.* . . . Illustrations de Hofer, Paris: Société littéraire de France, 1921.

Ae5   *Les Regrets,* édn du quatrième centenaire, Paris: La Connaissance, 1925.

Ae6   *Les Regrets de J. Du B. Angevin.* Introduction, notices et notes par le docteur Léon Cerf, Paris: R. Kieffer, 1927.*

Ae7   *Les Regrets,* ed. Albert Pauphilet, Paris: Centre de documentation universitaire, 1935.

Ae8   *Les Regrets,* préface de J. Porcher, Paris, 1942.*

Ae9   *Les Regrets.* Introduction et notes de M. Henri Guillemin, Geneva: Edn du Milieu du Monde, 1943.*

Ae10   *Les Regrets.* Préface et annotations par Augustin Jeanneau, Cholet: P. Hérault, 1944.*

Ae11   *Les Regrets.* Introduction de J. Isolle, Angers, 1944.*

Ae12   *Le Premier livre des Antiquitez de Rome* . . . Burins gravés par Albert Decaris [text revised by Henri Chamard], Paris: A la Voile latine, 1945.*

Ae13   *Les Antiquitez de Rome et les Regrets,* avec une introduction de E. Droz, Geneva: Droz, Lille: Giard, Paris: Minard, 1947 and 1960.
.1 Lytton Sells, A., *FS,* I (1947), 164–5.

Ae14   *Les Regrets.* Introduction de Pierre Grimal, Paris: Bibliothèque classique de Cluny, 1949; Paris: A. Colin, 1958.
.1 England, S. L., *YWMLS,* XII (1950), 29.

Ae15   *Les Regrets.* Introduction et notes de Jacques Levron, Paris: Delmas, 1955.

Ae16   *Les Regrets,* Paris: Laffont, 1958. (Collection les Cent chefs-d'œuvre de la langue française).

Ae17   *Les Regrets.* Présentation de Bernard de Fallois, Paris: Livre-club du libraire, 1959.

Ae18   *Les Regrets.* Texte établi par J. Jolliffe, introduit et commenté par M. A. Screech, Geneva: Droz (T.L.F.), 1966.
.1 Bowen, B. C., *MLR,* LXIII (1968), 476–7.
.2 Giraud, Y., *RHLF,* LXX (1970), 116–9.
.3 Lawton, H. W., *FS,* XXI (1967), 146–7.

.4 McFarlane, I. D., *YWMLS,* XXVIII (1966), 69.
.5 Price, G., *ZRP,* LXXXIII (1967), 437–8.
.6 Rekkers, B., *Het Franse Boek,* XXXVII (1967.), 115–6.
.7 Richter, M., *St. fr.,* XXXIV (1968), 133.

Ae19 *Les Regrets.* Précédés des *Antiquités de Rome* et suivis de la *Défense.* Préface de Jacques Borel. Edition établie par S. de Sacy, Paris: Hachette (Livre de Poche), 1967.

Ae20 *Les Regrets.* Choix de poèmes, avec une notice biographique, une notice historique et littéraire, un répertoire, un index, un lexique, des notes explicatives, des documents, des jugements, un questionnaire et des sujets de devoirs, par Y. Wendel-Bellenger, Paris: Classiques Larousse, 1969.
.1 Richter, M., *St. fr.,* XLI (1970), 334.

Ae21 *Les Regrets.* Edition critique publiée par Henri Chamard (Cinquième tirage revu et corrigé avec un cahier additionnel remis à jour en 1969 par Henri Weber), Paris: Didier (S.T.F.M.), 1970.

Ae22 *Les Antiquités, Les Regrets.* Chronologie et introduction par F. Joukovsky, Paris: Garnier-Flammarion, 1971.
.1 Richter, M., *St. fr.,* XLVI (1972), 139.

For an English translation of 6 of *Les Regrets* see Ba21

CRITICAL WORKS RELATING TO DU BELLAY

BOOKS AND THESES
DEVOTED PRINCIPALLY TO DU BELLAY
* * *

Ba1   Addamiano, Natale, *Delle opere poetiche francesi di Du B.
e delle sue imitazione italiane*, Cagliari: G. Leda, 1920;
Paris: Champion, 1921.
.1 Plattard, J., *RSS*, IX (1922), 91–2.

Ba2   Aebly, Hedwig, *Von der Imitation zur Originalität, Unter-
suchungen am Werke Bellays*, Zurich: J. Williger, 1942.*

Ba3   Amato, Modesto, *Ce que le manifeste de la Pléiade doit à
l'Italie*, Palermo: Trimarchi, 1917.*

Ba4   Ambrière, Francis, *J. Du B.*, Paris: Firmin-Didot, 1930.
Also appeared in part under same title in *Revue mondiale*,
192 (1929), 264–8.
.1 Tanquerey, F. J., *YWMLS*, I (1931), 48.

Ba5   Aubert de Poitiers, Guillaume, *Elegie sur le trespas de feu
J. Du B.*, Paris: Fédéric Morel, 1560. See also Aal, pp.
XXXVIII–XL; Ba36.

Ba6   Beaupère, Thérèse, 'La Rome de Du B.: étude archéologique,
historique et littéraire', Doctorat d'état, Univ. of Paris, 1955.*

Ba7   Belleau, Rémy, *Chant pastoral sur la mort de J. Du B.
Angevin*, Paris: Robert Estienne, 1560.*

Ba8   Beydts, Louis, *Les Jeux Rustiques. Trois poèmes de J. Du B.*,
musique de Louis Beydts, Paris: Heugel, c. 1931.*

Ba9   Bots, W. J. A., 'Erudition et naturel dans l'œuvre poétique de
Du B.', Doctorat d'Université de Paris, 1960.*

Ba10   . . . , *J. Du B. entre l'histoire littéraire et la stylistique.
Essai de synthèse*, Groningen: Van Denderen, 1970.
Doctoral thesis, Univ. of Leiden, 1970.*

Bourgo, Léo Le: see Le Bourgo, Léo.

Ba11   Boyer, Frédéric, *J. Du B.* [avec un choix de textes], Paris:
Seghers, 1958.
.1 McFarlane, I. D., *YWMLS*, XX (1958), 79.
.2 Mombello, G., *St. fr.*, XX (1963), 33 8.

Ba12   Brady, Margaret W. (Mrs Wells q.v.), 'Quelques aspects du Sonnet chez Marot, Ronsard et Du B.', M.A. thesis, Univ. of Southampton, 1969.

Ba13   Brevet, R., *Le Petit Lyré et J. Du B.*, Angers: Imprimerie centrale, 1967.

Ba14   Cates, Mary E., 'Du B.: idéalisme et sens poétique', M.A. thesis, Univ. of British Columbia, 1968.*

Ba15   Chamard, Henri, *J. Du B. (1522—1560)*, Lille: Librairie Le Bigot Frères, 1900. Doctoral thesis, Univ. of Paris, 1899—1900.
 .1 'Un Bibliophile', *RR*, I (Jan.–June 1901), 61–2.
 .2 Doutrepoint, A., *Musée belge* (15.11.1901), 267.*
 .3 Giraud, V., *RCC* (18.4.1901), 285.
 .4 Laumonier, P., *Annales littéraires et artistiques du Maine* (June 1901), 211–7.*
 .5 Pellisson, M., *Revue pédagogique* (15.12.1900), 638.*
 .6 Pergameni, H., *Revue de l'instruction publique en Belgique* (1902), 39.*
 .7 Vianey, J., *RHLF,* VIII (1901), 151–5.

 Clément, Louis: see Bb63.

Ba15a Deguy, Michel, *Tombeau de Du B.*, Paris: Gallimard, 1973.
 .1 Anon., *Times Literary Supplement* (14.9.73), 1051.

Ba16   Dickinson, Gladys, *Du B. in Rome*, Leiden: E. J. Brill, 1960.
 .1 Gloten, J. J., *BHR*, XXIV (1962), 266.
 .2 Lebègue, R., *RHLF*, LXII (1962), 600.
 ..3 McFarlane, I. D., *YWMLS,* XXII (1960), 69.
 .4 Sozzi, L., *St. fr.,* XIV (1961), 333.

Ba17   Ellain, Nicolas, *Elegiarum libri duo (ad Ioachimum Bellaium quo adhuc vivo eos scripsit),* Paris: 1560.

Ba18   François, Alexis, *Les Sonnets suisses de Du B.*, Lausanne: Librairie de l'Université, F. Rouge, 1946.
 .1 England, S. L., *YWMLS,* XI (1941–9), 44.
 .2 Rudler, G., *FS,* I (1947), 361–2.

Ba19   Garçon, Maurice, [Discours] *4ᵉ centenaire de Du B. à Liré le 26 juin 1960,* Paris: Firmin-Didot, 1960.*

Ba20   Gillot, Hubert, *La Querelle des anciens et des modernes en France. De la 'Défense' aux 'Parallèles des anciens et des modernes',* Paris: Champion, 1914.* Doctoral thesis, Univ. of Paris, 1913–4.

Ba21   Gottfried, Rudolf, *Six Sonnets from 'Les Regrets' by J. Du B. translated by R. G.,* Bloomington, Indiana: Corydon Press, 1944.*

Ba22   Grabowski, Tadeusz, *Petrarca i Du B. Kartkazdziejów Renesansú we Francyi,* Krakow, 1903.*

Ba23   Green, Susan M., 'A Critical Bibliography of J. Du B.', Bibliography submitted in part requirement for the Univ. of London Diploma in Librarianship by Susan Miriam Green. September, 1965.

Ba24   Griffin, Robert, *Coronation of the Poet, J. Du B.'s Debt to the Trivium,* Berkeley and Los Angeles: Univ. of California Publications in Modern Philology, 96, 1969.
.1 Cameron, K., *BHR,* XXXII (1970), 704–5.
.2 La Charité, C. R., *FR,* XLV (1971–2), 277–8.
.3 Nelson, R., *Ren. Q.,* XXIV (1971), 257–9.
.4 Richter, M., *St. fr.,* XLIII (1971), 132–3.
.5 Sharratt, P., *MLR,* LXVII (1972), 885–6.
.6 Stone, D., *MP,* LXVIII (1970–1), 382–3.
.7 Wiley, W. L., *Rom. Rev.,* LXIII (1972), 294–6.
.8 Wilson, D. B., *YWMLS,* XXXI (1969), 83.

Ba25   Guéroult, Guillaume, *La Lyre chrestienne avec la Monomachie de David et Goliath et plusieurs autres chansons spirituelles (par G. G.) nouvellement mises en musique par A. de Hauville,* Lyon, 1560.*

Ba26   Herval, René, *La Glorieuse maison Du B.,* Paris: J. Peyronnet & Cie, 1929.*

Ba27   Jolliffe, John W., 'The Influence of the *Regrets*', Ph.D. thesis, University College, Univ. of London, 1960.*

Ba28   Jose, C. E., 'Rhetoric and lyric poetry in Du B.', Ph.D. thesis, Univ. of Toronto, 1962.*

Ba29   Keating, L. Clark, *J. Du B.,* New York: Twayne Publ. Inc., 1971 (Twayne's World Authors Series, 162).

Ba30   Lafargue, A., *J. Du B., poète angevin du XVIe siècle (1525– 1560),* Angers, 1864.*

Ba31   Le Bourgo, Léo, *De Joach. Bellaii, latinis poematis,* Cognac: Librairie de G. Béraud, 1903. Doctoral thesis, Univ. of Rennes, 1902–3.

Ba32   Lenz, Konrad, 'Du B. und die Antike', Ph.D. thesis, Univ. of Marburg, 1924.*

Ba33   Levinson, Carla H., '*Les Antiquitez de Rome* étudiées d'après la théorie du travail poétique de J. Du B.', M.A. thesis, Univ. of Manitoba, 1966.*

Ba34   Lidforss, Volter E., *Observations sur l'usage syntaxique de Ronsard et de ses contemporains. . . . Avec une appendice contenant la 'Défense' de J. Du B.',* Lund: Gleerup, 1865.*

Ba35 Lüken, Erich, *Du B.'s 'Défense' in ihrem Verhältnis zu Sebillet's 'Art poétique'*, Oldenburg: A. Littmann, 1913. Doctoral thesis, Univ. of Kiel, 1913.*

Ba36 Marty-Laveaux, Charles, *Notice biographique sur J. Du B.*, Paris: A. Lemerre, 1867. (Extrait du premier volume de la *Pléiade Françoise)*

Ba37 McGovern, M. A., 'La Rhétorique dans les *Regrets* de Du B.', M.A. thesis, Queen's Univ. Belfast, 1970.*

Ba38 Merrill, Robert V., *The Platonism of J. Du B.*, Chicago UP, 1925.
.1 Harvitt, H., *MLN*, XLII (1926), 138–9.
.2 Tanquerey, F. J., *YWMLS*, I (1931), 48.

Ba39 Moisan, Jean-Claude, 'La Pensée religieuse dans l'œuvre de J. Du B.', Diplôme d'études supérieures, Univ. Laval, Quebec, 1967.*

Ba40 . . ., 'L'Humanisme dans l'œuvre française de J. Du B.', Doctoral thesis, Univ. of Grenoble, 1969.*

Ba41 Monnier, Eugène, *La Fontaine commémorative de J. Du B. à ériger à Ancenis (Loire-Inférieure)*, Paris: A. Lemerre, 1888.*

Ba42 Niord, Yvonne, 'A Study of the "imitation" of Italian Writers in J. Du B.'s Works', Ph.D. thesis, University College, Aberystwyth, Wales, 1958.*

Ba43 Nolhac, Pierre de, *Lettres de J. Du B. publiées pour la première fois d'après les originales*, Paris: Charavay, 1883. See also Bb181.

Ba44 Noo, Hendrik de, *Thomas Sebillet et son 'Art Poétique Françoys' rapproché de la 'Défense' de J. Du B.*, Utrecht: J. L. Beijers, 1927.
.1 Gaiffe, F., *RHLF*, XXXVIII (1931), 108–10.
2 Plattard, J., *RSS*, XIV (1927), 409–10.
.3 Tanquerey, F. J., *YWMLS*, II (1932), 40.

Ba45 Odoul, G., *Du B. sur la Montagne Sainte-Geneviève*, [Conférence faite à l'occasion du 4e centenaire de sa mort], Paris: Imprimerie royale, 1960.* Also in *La Montagne Sainte-Geneviève et ses abords*, 51 (June 1960).*

Ba46 Pflaenzel, Max, *Uber die Sonette des J. Du B. nebst eine Einleitung: Die Einführung des Sonetts in Frankreich*, Saalfeld (Saale): Wiedmannsche Hofbuchdr., 1898. Doctoral thesis, Univ. of Leipzig, 1898.

Ba47   Platt, Helen O., 'A Structural Study of Du B.'s *Jeux
        Rustiques*', Ph.D. thesis, Case Western Reserve Univ.,
        1971.* *DA*, XXXII (1971), 1524A–5A. See Bb195

Ba48   Plötz, Gustav C., *Etude sur J. Du B. et son rôle dans la
        réforme de Ronsard,* Berlin: Herbig, 1874. Doctoral thesis,
        Univ. of Halle ,1874.

Ba49   Rheault, R., 'J. Du B. et l'enrichissement du vocabulaire
        français', M.A. thesis, Univ. of Ottawa, 1965.*

Ba50   Richter, Bodo L. O., 'The Place of the Minor Italian Poets
        in the Works of Ronsard and Du B.', Ph.D. thesis, Univ. of
        Pennsylvania, 1951.* *DA*, XIV (1954), 973–4.
        .1 Silver, I., *Comp. Lit.,* VI (1954), 171.

Ba51   Rosenbauer, Andreas, *Uber Pierre Ronsard's Kunsttheoretische
        Ansichten* [Die poetischen Theorien der Plejade nach
        Ronsard und Du B. Ein Beitrag zur Geschichte der Re-
        naissancepoetik in Frankreich], Munich: Lippert & Co.,
        1895.* Doctoral thesis, Univ. of Munich, 1895.

Ba52   Saba, Guido, *La poesia di J. Du B.,* Messina-Firenze: G.
        d'Anna, 1962.
        .1 Antonioli, R., *RHLF,* LXIV (1964), 97–8.
        .2 Harvey, L. E., *MLN,* LXXVIII (1963), 546–50.
        .3 Lawton, H. W., *FS,* XVII (1963), 359–60.
        .4 del Missier, *Nuova Antologia,* 489 (1963), 547–9.
        .5 Mumford, I., *MLR,* LXIII (1968), 704–6.
        .6 Sozzi, L., *St. fr.,* XXIII (1964), 334.

Ba53   Sainati, Augusto, *Iacopo Sannazaro e J. Du B.,* Pisa:
        E. Spoerri, 1915.*

Ba54   Sanadon, N. E., *Epitaphe d'un petit chien en vers françois*
        [par J. Du B.] *et latins* [par N. E. Sanadon], S.l. n.d.*

Ba55   . . . , *Vers françois* [par J. Du B.] *et latins* [par Le P.N.E.
        Sanadon] *sur la mort d'un petit chat,* S.l. n.d.*

Ba56   Sandre, Thierry, *Du B. – les Amours de Faustine.* Poésies
        latines traduites pour la première fois et publiées avec une
        introduction et des notes par Thierry Sandre, Amiens:
        Malfère (Bibliothèque du Hérisson), 1923.
        .1 Mange, E., *Mercure de France,* CLXVI (Aug. 1923), 194–5.

Ba57   Satterthwaite, Alfred W., 'Spenser, Ronsard and Du B.: a
        comparative study', Ph.D. thesis, Harvard Univ. 1955–6.*

Ba58   . . . , *Spenser, Ronsard and Du B.: A Renaissance Comparison,*
        Princeton UP, 1960.
        .1 Arthos, J., *Symposium,* XV (1961), 303–5.
        .2 Caffin, D. J. O., *AUMLA,* (18.11.62), 248–50.

.3 Ellrodt, R., *Etudes anglaises,* XIV (1961), 237–8.
.4 Gleason, J. B., *Thought,* XXXVI (1961), 460–2.
.5 Lawton, H. W., *FS,* XVI (1962), 174–6.
.6 McFarlane, I. D., *YWMLS,* XXII (1960), 70; XXIII (1961), 60.
.7 McNeir, W. F., *MP,* LX (1962–3), 58–61.
.8 Mombello, G., *St. fr.,* XIX (1963), 142.
.9 Tellier, A. R., *RLC,* XXXVI (1962), 600–2.
.10 Thompson, P., *MLR,* LVII (1962), 84–5.

Ba59 Saulnier, Verdun L., *Les Antiquitez de Rome,* Paris: Centre de documentation universitaire, 1950.

Ba60 . . . , *Du B., l'homme et l'œuvre,* Paris: Hatier, 1951.
.1 Becker, G., *Information littéraire,* IV (1952), 73.
.2 Boase, A., *MLR,* L (1955), 243–4.
.3 Ch. G., *Revue belge,* XXX (1952), 565.
.4 Dédéyan, C., *Nouvelles littéraires,* 1270, 3 (1952).
.5 Desonay, F., *BHR,* XIII(1951), 395–7.
.6 England, S. L., *YWMLS,* XIII (1951), 36.
.7 Fonsny, J., *Et. class.,* XX (1952), 276.
.8 Frame, D., *Rom. Rev.,* XLIII (1952), 213–5.
.9 Jourda, P., *RHLF,* LIV (1954), 233–4.
.10 Spoerri, T., *Erasmus,* V (1952), 270–2.

Ba61 Schwaderer, Richard, *Das Verhältnis des Lyrikers J. Du B. zu seinen Vorbildern (Probleme der "imitation"),* Würzburg, 1968. Doctoral thesis, Univ. of Würzburg, 1968.

Ba62 Screech, Michael A., 'The Poetry of J. Du B.', Ph.D. thesis, Univ. of Birmingham, 1960.*

Ba63 Séché, Léon, *J. Du B.,* Paris: Didier, 1880.

Ba64 . . . , *Recherches sur la Pléiade, J. Du B. et la Bretagne Angevine,* [Paris?], 1900.*

Ba65 Smulders, Elizabeth, 'The Defence and Glorification of the French Language. Translated by E. S.', Ph.D. thesis, Pretoria, 1935.*

Ba66 Sutherland, G. M., 'Etude littéraire comparée de la poésie latine et française de J. Du B.', Doctoral thesis, Univ. of Paris, 1952.*

Ba67 Turnèbe, Adrien; Claude d'Espence; Léger du Chesne, *In Ioachimum Bellaium Andinum poetam clarissimum doctorum virorum Carmina et Tumuli,* Paris: Fédéric Morel, 1560.*

Ba68 Turquet, Gladys M., *The Defence & Illustration of the French Language . . . Translated . . . by Gladys M. Turquet,* London: Dent, 1939.*
.1 England, S. L., *YWMLS,* X (1940), 49.
.2 Orr, J., *MLR,* XXXIV (1939), 638.

Ba69 Vianey, Joseph, *'Les Antiquitez de Rome' de J. Du B.*,
      Bordeaux: Feret et fils, 1901. See Bb283.
      .1 Séché, L., *RR*, II (1902), 67.

Ba70 . . . , *Les Sources italiennes de 'L'Olive'*, Mâcon: Protat,
      1901. Also in *Histoire comparée de littérature* (Paris), VI
      (1901), 71–104.
      .1 Séché, L., *RR*, I (Jan.–June 1901), 285.

Ba71 . . . , *Les 'Regrets' de Du B.*, Paris: Malfère, 1930.
      .1 Jourda, P., *RHLF*, XL (1933), 122.
      .2 Plattard, J., *RSS*, XVII (1931), 187.
      .3 Tanquerey, F. J., *YWMLS*, III (1933), 49.

Ba72 Villey, Pierre, *Les Sources italiennes de la 'Défense'*, Paris:
      Champion, 1908. Also a selection of chapters in *RR*, X
      (1909), 11–55.
      .1 Norton, G., *MLN*, XXIV (1909), 191–2.
      .2 Sturel, R., *RHLF*, XVII (1910), 863–6.

Ba73 Ziemann, Georg, *Vers- und Strophenbau bei J. Du B.*,
      Königsberg, 1913. Doctoral thesis, Univ. of Königsberg,
      1913.

ARTICLES AND CHAPTERS OF BOOKS
DEVOTED MAINLY TO DU BELLAY

* * *

Bb1   Addamanio, Natale, 'Quelques sources italiennes de la
      Défense de J. Du B.', *RLC,* III (1923), 177–89.

Bb2   Adler, Alfred, 'Du B.'s *Antiquitez* XXXI. Structure and
      Ideology', *BHR,* XIII (1951), 191–5.
      .1 England, S. L., *YWMLS,* XIII (1951), 36.

Bb3   Allem, Maurice, 'Discours', read at banquet given 18.12.22 by
      the Société des Artistes angevins in collaboration with *La
      Muse française.* An account is given in *La Muse française*
      (10.1.23).*

Bb4   Ambrière, Francis, 'Rencontre de J. Du B. et de Ronsard',
      Revue mondiale, 192 (1929), 179–83.
      See also Ba4

Bb5   Amsler, Roger, and André Bruel, 'La Chétive existence de
      J. Du B.', *Aesculape* (July 1931), 177–81.*

Bb6   Andrieux, Maurice, 'Du B.', in *Les Français à Rome,* Paris:
      grandes études historiques, 1968, pp. 68–72.

Bb7   Anon., [Request for information about Du B.'s threatened
      lawsuit against French publishers], *RR,* I (Jan.–June 1901),
      63.

Bb8   Anon., [Le Liseur], 'J. Du B. à Rome', *RR,* XIV, 13 ^{e}
      année (Jan.–Mar. 1913), 58.

Bb9   Anon., 'La Surdité de J. Du B.', *Chroniques médicales* (1923),
      10.*

Bb10 Arens, John C., 'Du B.'s sonnet "Face le ciel". Adapted by
      Nicholas Grimald', *Papers on English Language and Literature,*
      I (1965), 77–8.

Bb11 Baillet, Adrien, 'Du B.', in *Jugemens des Sçavans sur les
      principaux ouvrages des auteurs,* Paris, 1685.* Edited by La
      Monnoye, Paris: 1722, vol. IV, pp. 412–4. See Bdl49.

Bb12   Bazin, René, 'Discours', read at banquet given 18.12.22 by the Société des Artistes angevins in collaboration with *La Muse française.* An account is given in *La Muse française* (10.1.23).*

Bb13   Belleuvre, P., 'La Famille Du B.', *Revue Anjou,* I, 1 (1856), 72–89, 200–21; and I, 2 (1856), 83–97.*

Bb14   Belloc, Hilaire, 'J. Du B.', in *Avril, being essays on the poetry of the French Renaissance,* London: Duckworth, 1904, pp. 151–94.

Bb15   Belowski, Eleonore, 'Du B. und Lukrez', in *Lukrez in der französischen Literatur der Renaissance,* Berlin: Emil Ebering, 1934, pp. 36–45. Doctoral thesis, Danzig Technische Hochschule, n.d.

Bb16   Bernard, Jean M., 'Les *Jeux Rustiques* de Du B.', *Revue critique des idées,* XXI (1913), 403–14.*

Bb17   Bertrand, Anthoine de, [Setting of *Olive* 58], in Bd17. See also Be250.

Bb18   Besnier, Charles, 'Sur les rencontres de Pierre de Ronsard et de J. Du B.', *Information littéraire,* XIV (1962), 79–86.

       Bever, Adolphe Van: see Van Bever, Adolphe.

Bb19   Billy, A., 'Sainte-Beuve et la "douceur angevine" ', *Le Figaro littéraire* (10.3.56), 2.*

Bb20   Blanchet, Adrien, 'La Faustine des *Poemata* de Du B.', *Académie des Inscriptions et Belles-Lettres* (21.11.24), 320.*

Bb21   . . . , 'Une Faustine à Rome au milieu du XVIe siècle', *Aréthuse,* II, 7 (Apr. 1925), 41–9.*

Bb22   Blordier-Langlois, 'Sur quelques écrivains de l'Anjou: J. Du B.', *Mem. Soc. Angers,* I (1831–4), 423–63.*

Bb23   Blümenfeld, W., ['J. Du B.'], in *Les Poètes de la Renaissance française,* Leningrad, 1938.*

       Boniface, Joseph-Xavier: see Saintine, X. B.

Bb24   Bordier, Jules, 'Le Petit Lyré, sonnet [paroles de] J. Du B. Musique de Jules Bordier', in *Œuvres choisies de J. Du B.,* ed. Camille Ballu, Paris: Revue illustrée des Provinces de l'Ouest, 1894.*

Bb25   Borel, Jacques, 'Du B. poète du retour', *Critique,* 242 (1967), 619–30.*

Bb26   Bots, W. J. A., 'L'Expression politique chez Du B.', *Levende Talen* (1965), 660–71.*

Bb27 ..., 'La Fonction de l'eau dans l'univers poétique de Du B.', *Levende Talen* (1967).*

Bb28 Boulenger, Jacques, 'Des vers latins de Du B. inconnus', *HR*, IV (1937), 208.

Bb29 Bourdeaut, A., 'Du B. et Olive de Sévigné', *Mem. Soc. Angers*, XIII (1910), 1–54.*

Bb30 ..., 'Les Malestroit et les Du B.', *Mem. Soc. Angers*, XIV (1911), 9–88.* Also published as *Les Malestroit d'Oudon et les Du B. de Liré*, Angers: Grassin, 1911.*

Bb31 ..., 'La Jeunesse de Du B. Ses parents, ses amis, ses ennemis en Anjou', *Mem. Soc. Angers*, XV (1912), 5–225.*
.1 Plattard, J., *RSS*, I (1913), 449–51.

Bb32 Bourin, André, 'Il y a quatre cents ans Du B. publiait les *Regrets*', *Les Nouvelles littéraires* (16.1.58), 7.

Bb33 Boutang, Pierre, 'Du B. et sa *Défense*', *Aspects de la France* (21.12.49 & 4.1.50).*

Bb34 Bruel, André, 'Essai sur le sentiment de la patrie dans l'œuvre de J. Du B.', *Mem. Soc. Angers*, V (1930), 159–71.* Also Angers: Bruel, 1931.*

Bb35 ..., 'Les Cousines de J. Du B., abbesses de Nyoiseau', *Mem. Soc. Angers*, IX (1934), 149–70.* Also Angers: Bruel, 1935.

   ... : see Bb5.

Bb36 Brunetière, Ferdinand, 'De Du B. jusqu'à Malherbe', in Bd25, pp. 35–56.

Bb37 ..., 'Discours [prononcé à l'inauguration de la statue de J. Du B. à Ancenis, le 2 septembre, 1894]', *Débats roses*, Ancenis (3.9.1894).* Also in *Discours académiques*, Paris: Perrin & cie., 1901.* Also in *Recueil des discours, rapports et pièces diverses lus dans les séances publiques et particulières de l'Académie française*, Paris: Firmin-Didot, 1895, pp. 853–70.

Bb38 ..., 'J. Du B. (1525–1560)', *RDM*, III (1900), 66–77; (1.2.1901), 660–76.

Bb39 Brunot, Ferdinand, 'La Première édition lyonnaise du *Discours de Du B. sur le faict des quatre estats du Royaume* (1567)', *RPFP*, VIII (1894), 89–100.

Bb40 Busson, Henri, 'Pamphagus. [Sources of Du B.'s Pamphagus]', *BHR*, XIV (1952), 289–93.
.1 England, S. L., *YWMLS*, XIV (1952), 43.

Bb41   Butler, H. E., 'J. Du B.', *Anglo-French Review,* II, 2
       (15.9.19), 136—40.

Bb42   Cacudi, N., 'Du B. a Roma', *Rassegna di studi francesi* (Jan.—
       March 1922).*

Bb43   Caldarini, Ernesta, 'Nuove fonti italiane dell'*Olive* ', *BHR,*
       XXVII (1965), 395—434.
       .1 McFarlane, I. D., *YWMLS,* XXVII (1965), 62.
       .2 Pastore-Stocchi, M., *St. fr.,* XXVI (1965), 340.

Bb44   Cameron, Alice, 'A Note on Desportes and Du B.', *MLN,*
       L (1935), 378—80.

Bb45   Cary, Henry F., 'Du B.', in *The Early French Poets,* London:
       A. M. Philpot, 1923, pp. 51—62.

Bb46   Castan, Félix, 'The realm of the imaginary in Du B./Ronsard
       and Du Bartas/La Ceppède', *Yale French Studies,* XLVII
       (1972), 110—23. Translated by W. F. Panici.

Bb47   Castex, Jean, 'Un ennemi politique de J. Du B.: Charles
       Carafa, évêque de Comminges', *Revue de Comminges,* 3 ^{e}
       et 4e trimestres (1959).*

Bb48   Chamard, Henri, 'Sur un passage de la *Défense*', *RHLF,* IV
       (1897), 160.

Bb49   . . . , 'Sur une page obscure de la *Défense*', *RHLF,* IV
       (1897), 239—45.

Bb50   . . . , 'La Date et l'auteur du "Quintil Horatien" ', *RHLF,* V
       (1898), 54—71.

Bb51   . . . , 'L'Invention de l'Ode et le différend de Ronsard et de
       Du B.', *RHLF,* VI (1899), 21—54.

Bb52   . . . , 'Un ancien exemplaire de J. Du B. [conservé à la
       Bibliothèque de l'Université de Paris] ', *Revue des biblio-
       thèques,* XIX (1909), 154—8.

Bb53   . . . , 'J. Du B. Bibliographie des *Regrets*', *Revue de l'en-
       seignement secondaire des jeunes filles* (1.1.28).*

Bb54   . . . , 'Bibliographie de J. Du B. *(Regrets)* et de Ronsard
       (Bergerie, Hymnes)', *Revue de l'enseignement secondaire des
       jeunes filles* (1.4.33 & 15.4.33).*

Bb55   . . . , 'L'Enfance et la jeunesse de J. Du B.', *Bull. Soc. Cholet*
       (1934), 147—55.*

Bb56   . . . , 'J. Du B. à Poitiers', in *Mélanges . . . J. Vianey,* Paris:
       Les Presses françaises, 1934, pp. 133—8. Extract from Bd36.

Bb57   . . . , 'Bibliographie de J. Du B. *(Regrets)*', *Revue de
       l'enseignement secondaire des jeunes filles* (Dec. 1939).*

Bb58 ....' Bibliographie des éditions de J. Du B.', *BBB* (1949), 400–15, 445–63.

Bb59 Chambers, Frank M., 'Lucan in the *Antiquitez de Rome*', *PMLA*, LX (1945), 937–48.

Bb60 Charaux, A., 'La Renaissance littéraire en France. Du B., Ronsard', *Etudes franciscaines*, VI (Dec. 1901)*; VII (March 1902), 272–81; VII (May 1902), 520–33; VIII (1902).*

Bb61 Chevaldin, L. E., 'Note philologique: "Mon Loyre Gaulois" dans J. Du B.', *Bulletin de la Faculté des Lettres de Poitiers*, XI (1893), 98–100.*

Bb62 Chocheyras, J., 'En marge de la *Défense*, Pierre Saliat; une préface critique de 1537', *BHR*, XXVIII (1966), 675–9.
.1 Jodogne, P., *St. fr.*, XXXII (1967), 335.
.2 McFarlane, I. D., *YWMLS*, XXVIII (1966), 65.

Bb63 Clément, Louis, 'Le Poète courtisan de J. Du B.', *RR*, V, 4ᵉ année (Nov.–Dec. 1904), 225–65. Also published separately, Paris: Revue de la Renaissance, 1905.

Bb64 Cohen, Gustave, 'Le Héraut d'armes de la Pléiade, Du B., Angevin', *Année propédeutique*, XI–XII (1952).*

Bb65 Cohen, Marcel, 'Quatre cents ans de défense et illustration', *Les Lettres françaises* (2.8.51).*

Bb66 Colletet, Guillaume, 'La Vie de J. Du B.', *RR*, XIII, 12ᵉ année (Apr.–June & July–Sept. 1912), 83–103, 165–70.

Bb67 Crosnier, A., '*Les Regrets* de J. Du B.', *Revue des Facultés catholiques de l'Ouest*, III (1894), 727–56.*

Bb68 Crouslé, L., 'Sur la *Défense*', *Instruction publique* (1886), 83.*

Bb69 Dallinges, L., 'Présence de la maladie et de la mort dans l'œuvre de Du B.', *Domaine suisse*, II (June–July 1956), 47–61.*

Bb70 Dassonville, Michel, 'De l'unité de la *Défense*', *BHR*, XXVII (1965), 96–107.
.1 Jodogne, P., *St. fr.*, XXVIII (1966), 132.
.2 McFarlane, I. D., *YWMLS*, XXVII (1965), 61.

Bb71 Davies, J. H. V., 'J. Du B. and the Pléiade', *Nine*, VII (Aut. 1951), 153–9. Special issue devoted to "Renaissance Poetry, Studies and Translations".

Bb72 Deger, Ernst, '*Les Regrets* von J. Du B. in der Schule', *Die neueren Sprachen*, XI (1962), 461–9.
.1 Waltz, M., *St. fr.*, XXVI (1965), 340.

Bb73 . . . , 'Die Heimatsonett von Du B.', *Praxis des neusprachlichen Unterrichts,* XIV (1967), 16–22.*

Bb74 Dennis, Holmes V. M., 'A Note on Horace and Du B.', *Classical Philology,* XXVI (1931), 326.

Bb75 Derème, Tristan, 'J. Du B.', *La Muse française* (10.2.24), 77–81. Special issue of *La Muse française* entitled "Ronsard et la Pléiade". See also account of Derème's part in the banquet given 18.12.22 by the Société des Artistes angevins in collaboration with *La Muse française,* in *La Muse française* (10.1.23).*

Bb76 Derocquigny, J., 'Quelques notes à la défense de Du B.', *RHLF,* XI (1904), 652–3.

Bb77 Deschamps, Gaston, 'J. Du B. – *L'Olive*', *RCC,* X (1902), 782–90.

Bb78 Duhem, Jules, 'Le Premier poète de l'aviation; essai sur les éditions de Sannazar, de Tansillo, et de J. Du B.', *BBB* (1946), 157–63.

Bb79 Elcock, W. D., 'English Indifference to Du B.'s *Regrets*', *MLR,* XLVI (1951), 175–84.
.1 England, S. L., *YWMLS,* XIV (1952), 43.

Bb80 Espiner-Scott, Janet, 'Some notes on Du B.', *MLR,* XXXVI (1941), 59–67.

Bb81 Feugère, Fernand, 'Du B. notre "préfondateur" ', *Défense de la langue française,* XXXV (Dec. 1966), 3–4.*

Bb82 Foulché-Delbosc, R., 'Notes sur le sonnet "Superbi colli", *Revue hispanique,* XI (1904), 225–43. See Be183.

Bb83 François, C. R., 'Cinq sonnets de *L'Olive* ou la clé d'une énigme', *BHR,* XV (1953), 215–9.
.1 England, S. L., *YWMLS,* XV (1953), 43.

Bb84 François, Michel, 'Le Quatrième centenaire de la *Défense*', *BHR,* XII (1950), 146–8.

Bb85 Françon, Marcel, 'J. Du B. et Rabelais', *FM,* XXI, 1 (Jan. 1953), 9–11.

Bb86 . . . , 'Influences des "Chroniques gargantuines" sur Ronsard et sur Du B.', *SP,* L (1953), 144–8.

Bb87 . . . , 'Le Folklore dans l'œuvre de J. Du B.', *Bulletin folklorique d'Ile de France* (July–Sept. 1955).*

Bb88 . . . , 'J. Du B.', in Bd71, pp. 79–82.

Bb89 . . . , 'J. Du B. and the *rime en écho*', *Romance Notes,* XI (1969–70), 153–5.

Bb90   Frémy, P., 'Texte commenté: J. Du B.; "D'un vanneur de
        blé aux vents" ', *Les Humanités* (Classe de lettres, Sections
        modernes) (Nov. 1965).*

Bb91   Froger, L., 'Les Hommes de lettres au XVIe siècle dans le
        diocèse du Mans', *RR,* IV, 3e année (Jan. and Feb.–Mar.
        1903), 47–54, 117–21.

Bb92   Fucilla, Joseph G., 'Sources of Du B.'s *Contre les
        Pétrarquistes*', *MP,* XXVIII (1930–1), 1–11.
        Also in Bd72, pp. 165–83.
        .1 Tanquerey, F. J., *YWMLS,* II (1932), 40.

Bb93   . . . , 'A sonnet in Du B.'s *Antiquitez de Rome*', *MLN,* LXI
        (1946), 260–2. Also in Bd72, pp. 185–8.

Bb94   Gallotti, Jean, 'Une journée de J. Du B.', *Les Nouvelles
        littéraires* (8.9.60), 2.

Bb95   Gambier, Henri, 'J. Du B.', in Bd74, pp. 89–114.

Bb96   Garanderie, P. de la, 'Du B. et le sonnet français. (Pour le
        IVe centenaire de la mort de J. Du B.)', *Mem. Soc. Angers,*
        VIIIe série, 4 (1960), 57–74.*
        .1 Mombello, G., *St. fr.,* XVII (1962), 335.

Bb97   Garçon, Maurice, 'Du B. en Anjou', *Les Nouvelles lit-
        téraires* (30.6.60), 4.

Bb98   Gilson, Etienne, 'Du B., Ronsard et nous', *Les Lettres
        françaises* (26.5.60), 1, 5.*

Bb99   Glatigny, Michel, 'Du B., traducteur dans les *Jeux Rustiques*',
        Information littéraire, XVIII (1966), 33–41.
        .1 McFarlane, I. D., *YWMLS,* XXVIII (1966), 70.

Bb100   Glauser, Alfred, 'Du B. et Belleau, ou les petites
        inventions', in *Le Poème-symbole de Scève à Valéry,*
        Paris: Corti, 1967, pp. 81–107.
        .1 Jeanneret, M., *BHR,* XXX (1968), 407–8.
        .2 Weinberg, B., *MLQ,* XXXI (1970), 373–4.
        .3 Wilson, D. B., *YWMLS,* XXIX (1967), 49.

Bb101   Gourmont, Remy de, 'Du B. grammairien', in *Promenades
        philosophiques,* I, Paris: Sociétés du Mercure de France, 1905,
        pp. 315–26.

Bb102   Groos, René, 'En marge des *Regrets.* Un sonnet "oublié" ',
        Les Humanités (Classe de lettres) (Oct. 1955).*

Bb103   Guérin, Charles, 'Comment Ronsard et Du B. disent leur
        découragement', *La Pensée catholique,* XXVIII (1955),
        102–9.*

Bb104 Hallays, André, 'Le "petit lyré" de J. Du B.', *Journal des débats* (24.5.12), 1.*

Bb105 . . . , 'J. Du B.', in *A travers la France, en flânant. De Bretagne en Saintonge,* Paris, 1930, pp. 91–100.

Bb106 Hanse, Joseph, 'Notes pour servir à l'analyse d'un sonnet de Du B.', *Ét. class.,* V (1936), 212–7.

Bb107 Hennion, Horace, ['Du B.'], *Dépêche* (25.11.22).* Also in *Journal d'Indre-et-Loire* (26.11.22).* See also *La Muse française* (10.1.23).*

Bb108 Henriot, E., 'La Résurrection de J. Du B.',*Le Temps* (29.5.30).*

Bb109 Heredia, Jcsé-Maria de, 'La Belle Viole' [sonnet], in *Les Trophées:* Le Moyen Age et la Renaissance. Sonnet first published in *RDM* (1.2.1893), 660. See also reference to this sonnet in Bb97. The sonnet was apparently a reply to a request by Léon Séché, who wanted poems composed in honour of Du B.

Bb110 . . . , [Discours prononcé à l'inauguration de la statue de J. Du B. à Ancenis, le 2 septembre 1894], in *Recueil des discours, rapports et pièces diverses lus dans les séances publiques et particulières de l'Académie française,* Paris: Firmin-Didot, 1895, pp. 847–52.

Bb111 Herriot, Edouard, 'J. Du B.', *Le Monde* (23.12.49).* [Discours aux Archives Nationales, 21.12.49]

Bb112 . . . , 'Le Manifeste de J. Du B.', *Cahiers français d'information,* I (1.5.50), 3–5.*

Bb113 . . . , 'Défense et Illustration de la langue française', *Revue Hommes et Mondes,* XII (May 1950), 1–6.*

Bb114 Hervier, Marcel, 'Du B.', in *Les Ecrivains français jugés par leurs contemporains,* Paris: Librairie Classique Paul Delaplane, 1911, pp. 21–6.

Bb115 Hill, Raymond T., 'The Influence of the *Noie* on the Poetry of J. Du B.', in *Essays in Honour of Albert Feuillerat,* New Haven: Yale UP, 1943, pp. 85–92.
.1 Lytton Sells, A., *MLR,* XL (1945), 131–3.

Bb116 Holyoake, S. J., 'J. Du B.'s *Défense*', in *An Introduction to French Sixteenth-Century Poetic Theory,* Manchester UP, 1972, pp. 66–126.

Bb117 Horrent, Jacques, 'Défense et illustration de *L'Olive*', *Cahiers d'analyse textuelle,* X (1968), 93–116.

Bb118 Howarth, W. D. and Ch. L. Walton, 'Du B. (*Regrets* XXXI. Explication littéraire)', in *Explications. The Technique of French Literary Appreciation*, London U.P., 1971, pp. 25–40.

Bb119 Ioachimescu, Th., 'Du B. intre tradiţie şi inovaţie', in *Omagiu lui Iorgu Iordan*, Bucharest, 1958, pp. 413–25.* (Du B. between tradition and innovation).

Bb120 Jacoubet, Henri, 'Pourquoi Du B. s'est-il rajeuni? ', *Mem. Acad. Toulouse*, 12ᵉ série, X (1932), 25–31.

Bb121 . . . , 'A propos de deux vers de Du B. Ce n'est pas Du B., c'est Ronsard qui s'est rajeuni', *Mem. Acad. Toulouse*, 12ᵉ série, XI (1933), 183–93.
.1 Lawton, H. W., *YWMLS*, V (1935), 53.

Bb122 Janik, Dieter, 'Die Enstehung der Ode - die *Vers lyriques* Du Bs', in Bd111, pp. 16–24.

Bb123 . . . , 'Die letzten panegyrischen Oden Ronsards und Du Bs', in Bd111, pp. 63–6.

Bb124 Jasinski, René, 'Sur la composition des *Regrets*', in *Mélanges . . . Abel Lefranc*, Paris: Droz, 1936, pp. 339–48.

Bb125 Jeanneau, Augustin, '*L'Olive* de J. Du B.', *Bull. Soc. Cholet* (1940), 27–31.*

Bb126 . . . , 'J. Du B. et les *Regrets*', *Bull. Soc. Cholet* (1945–7), 109–20.*

Bb127 Jolliffe, John, 'Du B.'s *Hymne chrestien*', *BHR*, XXII (1960), 356–9.
.1 McFarlane, I. D., *YWMLS*, XXII (1960), 69–70.
.2 Sozzi, L., *St. fr.*, XIII (1961), 140.

Bb128 . . . , 'Fédéric Morel and the works of Du B.', *BHR*, XXII (1960), 359–61.
.1 McFarlane, I. D., *YWMLS*, XXII (1960), 69–70.

Bb129 . . . , 'Further notes on Du B.', *BHR*, XXVIII (1966), 112–22.
.1 Campagnoli, R., *St. fr.*, XXXI (1967), 129–30.
.2 McFarlane, I. D., *YWMLS*, XXVIII (1966), 69.

Bb130 Keating, L. Clark, 'Promise and performance. Du B.'s *Défense*', *FR*, XLV (Special issue, 3), (1971), 77–83.

Bb131 Kiesel, F., 'Lamartines *l'Isolement* und Du Bs *l'Idée*', *Zeitschrift für französischen und englischen Unterricht*, XIII (1915), 451–2.*

Bb132 Krappe, Alexander H., 'Une source virgilienne de la *Défense* de Du B. (Livre II, Ch. 12)', *RSS*, XV (1928), 342–3.

Bb133 Krömer, Wolfram, 'Die Ursprünge und die Rolle der Sprachtheorie in Du B.'s *Défense*. (Zum Problem der Sprache ohne Klassiker in der Renaissance)', *Romanische Forschungen*, LXXIX (1967), 589—602.
.1 Drost, W., *St. fr.*, XL (1970), 140.

Bb134 Labracherie, Pierre, 'Le IVᵉ centenaire de la *Défense*', *Cahiers français d'information* (1.1.50).*

Bb135 Langeard, Paul, 'J. Du B. à Louis des Masures: un sonnet oublié', *BBB*, n.s., 10ᵉ année (1931), 108—10.

Bb136 Lapp, John C., 'Mythological imagery in Du B.', *SP*, LXI (1964), 109—27.
.1 Campagnoli, R., *St. fr.*, XXX (1966), 541.
.2 McFarlane, I. D., *YWMLS*, XXVI (1964), 68.

Bb137 Laurent, M., 'Du B.: Folie des courtisans et des poètes (*Regrets* CXLIX)', *L'Ecole* (7.10.61), 97—8.*
.1 Olivero, A., *St. fr.*, XXII (1964), 137—8.

Bb138 . . . , 'Explication française. Du B., l'exil du poète (*Regrets* XVI)', *L'Ecole* (19.10.63).*

Bb139 . . . , 'Explication française. Du B., *Les Regrets* I ('Je ne veux point fouiller au sein de la nature. . . '), *L'Ecole* (3.10.64).*

Bb140 Lebègue, Raymond, 'Dans l'entourage de Du B.', *BHR*, IV (1944), 171—6.

Bb141 . . . , 'Les Concurrences poétiques au XVIᵉ siècle, Ronsard, Du B., Baïf', *Comptes rendus de l'Académie des inscriptions et belles-lettres* (1958—9), 339—45.*.
.1 Sozzi, L., *St. fr.*, XI (1960), 334.

Bb142 L[enient], C[harles], 'Du B.: 1525—1560', in *Les Poètes français: Recueil des chefs-d'œuvre de la poésie française depuis les origines jusqu'à nos jours*, avec une notice littéraire sur chaque poète . . . publié sous la direction de M. Eugène Crépet, Paris: Quantin, 1887, vol.II, pp. 55—62.*

Bb143 Léonetti, A., 'Le Sonnet du "Petit Lyré". Variations sur l'air marin', *Revue universitaire*, LVII (1948), 146—50.
See Bb169.

Bb144 Leroy, André, 'Une amitié littéraire: Ronsard et Du B.', in *Mélanges . . . Paul Laumonier*, Paris: Droz, 1935, pp. 219—42.

Bb145 Letessier, Fernand, 'Note sur la première rencontre de Ronsard et Du B.', *Revue universitaire*, LIX (1950), 85—7.

Bb146 Levallois, J., 'J. Du B.', *Instruction publique* (1881), 762, 780, 795.*

Bb147 Levron, Jacques, 'Du B. et la *Défense*', *Larousse mensuel* (Dec. 1949).*

Bb148 Listard, Charles, 'Etude sur Du B.', *Mémoires de l'Académie du Gard* (1862), 355–76.* Also publ. separately, Nîmes: Clavel-Ballivet, 1863.*

Bb149 Louis, F., 'Cinéma et enseignement littéraire (suite). 1. Un texte poétique de Du B.: "Heureux qui comme Ulysse . . . " ', *Entre nous.* Cahiers trimestriels de documentation et d'information (Apr.– June 1958).*

Bb150 Maddison, Carol H., 'Sources of Du B.'s *Les Louanges d'Amour*', *MLN*, LXXIII, (1958), 594–7.
.1 McFarlane, I. D., *YWMLS*, XXI (1959), 61.
.2 Sozzi, L., *St. fr.*, VIII (1959), 301.

Bb151 Madeleine, Jacques, 'Sur un exemplaire des œuvres françaises de J. Du B.', *Revue des bibliothèques*, XIX (1909), 159–66.

Bb152 Martel, T., 'L'Homme et l'œuvre [J. Du B.]', *Figaro* (16.12.22).*

Bb153 Martin, Tristan, 'Le Logis de J. Du B. à Liré', *Répertoire archéologique* (Anjou), (1868), 93–7.*

Bb154 Marty-Laveaux, Charles, 'J. Du B.', in Bd146, pp. 384–403.

Bb155 Mayer, C. A., 'Une plaquette contenant une ode de Du B.', *BHR*, XVII (1955), 284–5.

Bb156 McClelland, John, '*Les Antiquitez de Rome:* document culturel et politique', in *Culture et politique en France à l'époque de l'Humanisme et de la Renaissance,* Congrès de Turin et Venise (29 March – 3 April 1971).*
.1 Jodogne, P., *St. fr.*, XLIV (1971), 265–6.

Bb157 Menasci, Guido, 'J. Du B. à Rome', in *De Ronsard à Rostand,* Firenze: Saggi di letteratura francese, 1901, 37–45.

Bb158 Merrill, Robert V., 'A Note on the Italian Genealogy of Du B.'s *Olive,* Sonnet 113', *MP*, XXIV (1926–7), 163–6.

Bb159 . . . , 'Lucian and Du B.'s *Poète courtisan*', *MP*, XXIX (1931–2), 11–20.

Bb160 . . . , 'Considerations on the *Amours* of J. Du B.', *MP*, XXXIII (1935–6), 129–38.
.1 Lawton, H. W., *YWMLS*, VII (1937), 47.

Bb161 . . . , 'Jean Lemaire, Du B. and the second Georgic', *MLN*, LI (1936), 453–5.

Bb162 . . . , 'Du B.'s *Olive* 112 and the *Rime diverse*', *MLN,* LX (1945), 527–30.

Bb163 Messiaen, Pierre, 'La *Défense*', *Revue des Idées,* II (1904), 784–94.*

Bb164 Meyer, G., 'Texte commenté. Du B. *Regrets* VI', *Les Humanités* (Classe de lettres, Section classique), (Feb. 1968), 22–4.*

Bb165 Michajlov, A. D., 'Žoašen Dju Belle i Kleman Maro: O dvux perevodax iz Petrarki', *Filologičeskie nauki,* VI, 2 (1963), 199–203.*

Bb166 Mimin, P., 'Défense et illustration de la langue judiciaire selon J. Du B.', *Mem. Acad. Angers,* 8ᵉ série, IV (1960), 75–8.*
  .1 Mombello, G., *St. fr.,* XVII (1962), 335.

Bb167 Morçay, Raoul, and Armand Müller, 'J. Du B.', in Bd158, pp. 321–35.

Bb168 Moreau, Pierre, 'En marge de trois vers latins des *Regrets*', in *Mélanges . . . Henri Chamard,* Paris: Nizet, 1951, pp. 71–9.

Bb169 Mougeont J., and A. Léonetti, 'Lettres – à propos du Petit Lyré. Suite des variations sur l'*air marin*', *Revue universitaire,* LVIII (1949), 15–16. See Bb143.

Bb170 Moulié, Charles, 'J. Du B. à Rome: les amours de Faustine', *Revue critique des idées et des livres,* XXIX (25.8.20), 470–80.*

Bb171 Müller, Armand, 'Deux étoiles de la Pléiade: Du B. et Belleau', in Bd160, pp. 155–78.

Bb172 . . . , 'Du B. en Italie', *L'Ecole* (27.4.63).*

Bb173 Nagel, Heinrich, 'Die Strophenbildung Baïf's im Vergleich mit der Ronsard's, Du B.'s und Rémy Belleau's', *Archiv,* LXI (1879), 439–62.

Bb174 Navagero, Andrea, 'J. Du B. . . . Vœux rustiques', in *Andreae Naugerii Lusus* . . . [Translations and adaptations of the Lusus], Haarlem, 1947.*

Bb175 Nelson, C. E., 'Enumeration and Irony in the *Regrets* of Du B.', *FR,* XXXVI (1962–3), 260–75.
  .1 McFarlane, I. D., *YWMLS,* XXV (1963), 45.

Bb176 Nepveu, André, 'Un Angevin ami de J. Du B. – Jacques Bouju (1515–1577)', *Mem. Acad. Angers,* V (1961), 39.*
  .1 McFarlane, I. D., *YWMLS,* XXV (1963), 45.

Bb177 Neri, Ferdinando, 'Note ai *Regrets*', *Athenaeum* (Pisa), VII (1919), 185–93.* Also in *Letteratura e Leggende,* Turin: Chiantore, 1951, pp. 225–32.*

Bb178 Neubert, Fritz, 'Die Briefe J. Du Bs (1559)', *Die neueren Sprachen,* XIII, (1964), 268–83.
.1 Drost, W., *St. fr.,* XXV (1965), 140.

Bb179 Nicholas, B. L., 'The uses of the sonnet: Louise Labé and Đu B.', in *French Literature and its Background: The Sixteenth Century,* ed. J. Cruickshank, Oxford UP, 1968, pp. 98–116.
.1 Jodogne, P., *St. fr.,* XXXVIII (1969), 330–1.
.2 McFarlane, I. D., *FS,* XXIII (1969), 172–5.
.3 Pouilloux, Y. J., *RHLF,* LXX (1970), 115–6.
.4 Wilson, D. B., *YWMLS,* XXX (1969), 72.

Bb180 Nitze, W. A., 'The Sources of the Ninth Sonnet of *Les Regrets*', *MLN,* XXXIX (1924), 216–9.

Bb181 Nolhac, Pierre de, 'Documents nouveaux sur la Pléiade: Ronsard, Du B.', *RHLF,* I (1894), 49–51, and V (1899), 351–61. See Ba43.

Bb182 . . . , 'J. Du B. au Palais Farnèse', *Figaro* (16.12.22).*

Bb183 . . . , 'Un centenaire oublié: J. Du B.', *RDM,* XCII^e année, 7e période, XII (Nov. 1922), 71–86.

Bb184 Noot, Jan van der, [Sonnets translated from the Visions of Du B.] in *A Theatre for Voluptuous Worldlings 1569,* New York: Scholars' Facsimiles and Reprints, 1936, 1940.*

Bb185 Outrey, Amédée, 'J. Du B. et la fontaine de Véron', *RSS,* XIX (1932–3), 246–61. Also in *Bull. Soc. Sens,* XXXIX (1934–6), 249–64.
.1 Tanquerey, F. J., *YWMLS,* V (1935), 53.

Bb186 . . . , 'Recherches sur la maison habitée par J. Du B. au cloître Notre-Dame', *Bulletin de la Société de l'histoire de Paris et de l'Ile-de-France,* LXI (1934), 76–102.*

Bb187 Parent, Monique, 'Un trait caractéristique du style de Du B.: l'expression du mouvement', in *Mélanges . . . A. Henry,* Strasbourg, 1970, pp. 223–9.*
.1 Sharratt, P., *YWMLS,* XXXII (1970), 45.

Bb188 Parvi, Jerzy, 'O Polski wybór wierszy J. Du B.', *Twórczosc,* I (1962).* (On the Polish selection of J. Du B.'s verse.)

Bb189 Pater, Walter, 'J. Du B.', in *The Renaissance, Studies in Art and Poetry,* Portland, Maine: T. B. Mosher, 1902, pp. 107–21. Originally published under title *Studies in the History of the Renaissance,* London, 1873.

Bb190 Pavie, André, 'Sainte-Beuve et J. Du B.', in *Médaillons romantiques,* Paris: Librairie Emile Paul, 1909, pp. 173–94.
.1 Rouxière, J. de la, *RR,* X, 9e année (1909), 57.

Bb191 . . . , 'Un portrait romantique de J. Du B.', *Figaro* (16.12.22).*

Bb192 . . . , 'J. Du B., poète de France et d'Anjou', *Echo de Paris* (21.12.22).* •

Bb193 Perrotin, Léo, 'Pour Didon. Sur quatre vers d'Ausone traduits par J. Du B.', in *Mélanges . . . Paul Laumonier,* Paris: Droz, 1935, pp. 189–200.

Bb194 Pighi, G. B., 'Versioni da Du B.', *Il Verri* (Dec. 1959), 19–25.*
.1 Sozzi, L., *St. fr.,* XII (1960), 535.

Bb195 Platt, Helen O., 'Structure in Du B.'s *D.J.R.*', *BHR,* XXXV (1973), 19–37.

Bb196 Plattard, Jean, 'J. Du B. [Manifestations diverses à l'occasion de son 4e centenaire]', *RSS,* IX (1922), 302–3.

Bb197 . . . , 'Le Souvenir de J. Du B. [Plaque commémorative apposée à Paris, 13 impasse Chartrière]', *RSS,* XIII (1926), 308.

Bb198 Pompeati, A., 'La giovinezza di Du B. e l'Italia', *Marzocco* (22.1.21).*

Bb199 Pouvereau, Henry, 'A l'abbaye de Saint-Maur au XVIe siècle: les Du B.', *Le Vieux Saint-Maur* (Spring 1949).*

Bb200 Prestreau, G., 'Hommage à Du B. [Discours à Liré, 26.6.60]', *Mem. Acad. Angers,* 8e série, IV (1960), 79–91.* Also in *Bulletin de la Fédération des Sociétés Savantes de Maine-et-Loire* (1961).*
.1 Mombello, G., *St. fr.,* XVII (1962), 335.

Bb201 Raibaud, Gabriel, 'Glanes dans les *Regrets* de J. Du B.', *Revue universitaire,* XLIX (1940), 120–7.

Bb202 Rat, Maurice, 'La Faustine de J. Du B.', *RDM* (Jul.–Aug. 1967), 371–7.

Bb203 Raymond, Marcel, 'Ronsard et Du B.', *RHLF,* XXXI (1924), 573–603.

Bb204 Rehm, W., 'La Grandeur du rien. J. Du B.', in Bd184, pp. 77–107.

Bb205 Reichenberger, K., 'Das Italianerlebnis Du Bs: Die Thematik des *Songe* und seine Beziehung zur manierischen Ideenwelt', *ZRP,* LXXXII (1966), 261–6.
.1 Dierlamm, W., *St. fr.,* XXXVIII (1969), 333–4.
.2 McFarlane, I. D., *YWMLS,* XXVIII (1966), 69–70.

Bb206 Renwick, W. L., 'Mulcaster and Du B.', *MLR,* XVII (1922), 282–7.

Bb207 Révillout, Charles, 'Des derniers mois de J. Du B.', in *Mémoires lus à la Sorbonne en 1867*, Paris: Imprimerie impériale, 1867, pp. 375–408.* See Bd193.

Bb208 Rivière, Jacques, 'Portrait de J. Du B.', *NRF*, VII (Jan.–June 1912), 519-22. Also in *Nouvelles études*, 9ᵉ edn, Paris: Gallimard, 1947, pp. 29–31.*

Bb209 Rouault, Joseph, 'Larmes sur les soldats tombés en la bataille de St. Quentin, poème latin de J. Du B.', *Eurydice*, cahier 2 (Aut. 1933), no pagination.

Bb210 . . . , 'Découverte d'un important inédit latin de J. Du B.', *Eurydice*, cahier 6 (Dec. 1933), no pagination.

Bb211 . . . , 'La Philosophie humaniste de J. Du B. – regards sur la mort', *Eurydice*, cahier 7 (Jan.–Feb. 1934), no pagination.

Bb212 . . . , 'La Philosophie humaniste de J. Du B. – regards sur la vie', *Eurydice*, cahier 11 (Sept. –Oct. 1934), no pagination.

Bb213 . . . , 'L'Humanisme de J. Du B., Angevin, et l'amour de la nature', *Eurydice*, cahier 21 (May–June 1936), no pagination.

Bb214 . . . , 'L'Humanisme de J. Du B., Angevin, et le regret de la Patrie', *Revue des questions historiques*, CXXV (1936), 42–62.

Bb215 . . . , 'J. Du B. et Goethe, amoureux de Faustina, la belle Romaine', *Eurydice*, cahier 25 (Jan. 1937), no pagination.

Bb216 . . . , 'Une rencontre spirituelle de J. Du B. avec Pic de la Mirandole et saint Thomas More', *Eurydice*, Cahier 37 (Feb. 1939), 38–48.

Bb217 . . . , 'Le Dernier Hymne chrétien', *Eurydice* (1938–9).*

Bb218 Roy, Emile, 'Lettre d'un Bourgignon, contemporain de la *Défense*', *RHLF*, II (1895), 234–43. See Be92.

Bb219 . . . , 'Question sur un passage obscur de la *Défense*', *RHLF*, II (1895), 468.

Bb220 . . . , 'Charles Fontaine et ses amis; sur une page obscure de la *Défense*', *RHLF*, IV (1897), 412–22.

Bb221 Russell, Daniel, 'Du B.'s emblematic vision of Rome', *Yale French Studies*, XLVII (1972), 98–109.

Bb222 Ruutz-Rees, Caroline, 'Some debts of Samuel Daniel to Du B.', *MLN*, XXIV (1909), 134–7.

Bb223 . . . , 'A Coincidence explained', *MLN*, XXVI (1911), 159.

Bb224 Saint-Denis, E. de, 'Des vers latins de Hildebert aux *Antiquités* de J. Du B.', *Et. class.*, VIII, (1939), 352–8.

Bb225 Sainte-Beuve, Charles A., 'Anciens poètes français: J. Du B.',
RDM, XXIV (1840), 161–90.*. Also in *Tableau de la littérature française au XVIe siècle*, Paris: Charpentier, 1843,
pp. 333–64:

Bb226 . . . , 'Premier, deuxième, et troisième article' [on Aa1],
Journal des Savants (Apr. 1867), 205–21; (June 1867), 344–
59; (Aug. 1867), 483–503. Also in *Nouveaux Lundis*, XIII
(June 1867), 294–321; (Aug. 1867), 322–56.*

Bb227 Sainte-Marthe, Scévole de, '[Du B.]', in *Gallorum doctrina
illustrium Elogia*, Paris, 1958, p. 39. See Bd46.

Bb228 Saintine, X. B. (Pseud. of Joseph Xavier Boniface), [Epître
de J. Du B. à Erasme pour l'engager à venir se fixer en France.
Ces vers sont censés traduits d'une épître latine de J. Du B.],
in *Institut Royal de France. La Renaissance des lettres et
des arts sous François Ier*, Paris, 1822.*

Bb229 Samarin, Charles, 'Un document notarié sur J. Du B. (5.12.
1559)', in *Mélanges . . . Abel Lefranc*, Paris: Droz,1936,
pp. 349–53.

Bb230 Satterthwaite, Alfred W., 'Moral Vision in Spenser, Du B.,
and Ronsard', *Comp. Lit.*, IX (1957), 136–49.
.1 Nicholas, B. L., *St. fr.*, III (1957), 482.
.2 Sozzi, L., *St. fr.*, VI (1958), 484.

Bb231 Saulnier, Verdun L., 'Commentaire sur la *Complainte des
Satyres*', *AUP* (1948), 151–8.*

Bb232 . . . , 'Commentaires sur les *Antiquitez de Rome*', *BHR*,
XII (1950), 114–43.
.1 England, S. L., *YWMLS*, XII (1950), 29.

Bb233 . . . , 'Sur diverses amitiés de Maurice Scève. IV, Scève,
Du B. et les voyageurs', *BHR*, XII (1950), 233–4.
.1 England, S. L., *YWMLS*, XII (1950), 31.

Bb234 . . . , 'Introduction à l'étude de J. Du B.', *Information
littéraire* (Jan.–Feb. 1950), 1–7.*

Bb235 . . . , 'Sur deux poèmes des *Jeux Rustiques* de J. Du B.',
Revue universitaire, LIX (1950), 265–71.

Bb236 . . . , 'Brantôme et J. Du B.', *BBB*, n.s. (1951), 107–25.

Bb237 . . . , ' "Soucelle et Patrière". Deux poètes inconnus du
règne d'Henri II et la première réputation de J. Du B.',
BBB, n.s. (1952), 1–22.

Bb238 . . . , 'Sebillet, Du B., Ronsard – L'Entrée de Henri II à
Paris et la révolution poétique de 1550', in *Fêtes de la
Renaissance*, ed. Jean Jacquot, Paris: Edns du Centre
national de la Recherche Scientifique, 1956, pp. 31–59.

Bb239 . . . , 'Des vers inconnus de Bertrand Berger, et les relations du poète avec Dorat et Du B.', *BHR*, XIX (1957), 245–51.
.1 Giudici, E., *St. fr.*, III (1957), 481–2.

Bb240 . . . , 'J. Du B. et la poésie', *AUP*, XXXI (1961), 44–53.
.1 Sozzi, L., *St. fr.*, XVI (1962), 135.

Bb241 . . . , 'Du B. et son "Regret" latin de la patrie', in *Mélanges . . . Robert Guiette*, Antwerp: De Nederlandsche Boekhandel, 1961, pp. 271–81.
.1 Sozzi, L., *St. fr.*, XVII (1962), 335.

Bb242 . . . , 'Du B. voyageur', *Mem. Acad. Angers* (1962).*

Bb243 . . . , 'Itinéraire et aventures de Jean et Joachim Du Bellay dans leur voyage italien. (Documents inédits)', in *Mélanges . . . Jean-Marie Carré*, Paris; Didier, 1964, pp. 465–84. Also in *Folklore Studies in Honor of Arthur Palmer Hudson*, Chapel Hill, 1965. (*N. C. Folklore*, XIII, 1–2 (1965), Special Issue).*

Bb244 . . . , 'Un ami de J. Du B., Pierre Gilbert', *BHR*, XXVIII (1966), 26–31.
.1 McFarlane, I. D., *YWMLS*, XXVIII (1966), 70.
.2 Richter, M., *St. fr.*, XXXI (1967), 130.

Bb245 . . . , 'L'Elégie testamentaire de J. Du B.', in Bd143, pp. 113–22.

Bb246 Savette, P., 'A propos de J. Du B. et de P. de Ronsard', *Soc. de Saumur*, 72 (1934), 45–7.*

Bb247 . . . , 'J. Du B. et ses cousines "de Sévigné" ', *Soc. de Saumur*, 73 (1935), 21–4.*

Bb248 . . . , 'Une branche obscure, ignorée et contestée de la famille Du B. en Anjou. Les Du B. D'Athée en Longué et du Plessis-Thiour en Saint-Georges-des-Sept-Voies', *Soc. de Saumur*, 76 (1935), 22–34.

Bb249 . . . , 'De J. Du B. à Pierre de Ronsard. Olive de Sévigné et Hélène de Surgères', *Soc. de Saumur*, 77 (1936), 47–9.*

Bb250 . . . , 'Les Du B. de Champagne et leur rameau de Drouilly-en-Vendômois', *Soc. de Saumur*, 87 (1939), 16–22.*

Bb251 Schlegel, 'Variations sur les vers de Du B. "Heureux qui comme Ulysse, a fait un beau voyage" ', *Revue pédagogique*, LXV (Aug.-Sept. 1914), 185–93. (Discours prononcé à la distribution des prix du Lycée d'Angers, par M. Schlegel, professeur de Philosophie.)

Bb252 Schwaderer, Richard, 'Schöpferische "imitatio" bei Du B. Ein Jugendsonett und sein Vorbild', *Arcadia*, VI (1971), 245–56.

Bb253 Schweig, Günter, 'Zur Gedichtinterpretation auf der Oberstufe im Französischunterricht: Du B. "Heureux qui comme Ulysse . . . " ', *Die neueren Sprachen*, XVI (1967), 485–90.

Bb254 Séché, Léon, 'Sur la prononciation du nom de Joachim', *RR*, I (Jan.–June 1901), 8, 72.

Bb255 . . . , 'Les Origines de J. Du B.', *RR*, I, 2e année (Jan.–June 1901), 9–31.

Bb256 . . . , 'Vie de Joachim [Du B.] ', *RR*, I, 2e année (Jan.–June 1901), 73–93, 129–62.

Bb257 . . . , 'Sur la dame qui fut Olive', *RR*, I, 2e année (Jan.–June 1901), 239–41.

Bb258 . . . , 'Le Pays de J. Du B.', *RR*, II, 2e année (Feb.–Mar.; Apr.–May 1902), 82–93, 169–80, 213–33.

Bb259 . . . , [Question and reply on genealogy of Catherine d'Ancenis, cousin of Jeanne Sauvain, ancestor of J. Du B.], *RR*, IV, 3e année (Apr.–May; June–Sept. 1903), 126, 185.

Bb260 . . . , 'L'Olive de J. Du B.', *RR*, XI, 10e année (Jan.–Mar. 1910), 1–21.

Bb261 . . . , 'La Famille de J. Du B.', *RR*, XI, 10e année (Apr.–June 1910), 105–6. Also in *Anjou historique*, II (1901–2), 289–93.

Bb262 Silver, Isidore, 'Pindaric parallelism in Du B. – a proof of his independent imitation of Pindar', *FR*, XIV (1940–1), 461–72.

Bb263 . . . , 'Ronsard imitator of Du B.', *SP*, XXXVIII (1941), 165–87.

Bb264 . . . , 'Did Du B. know Pindar? , *PMLA*, LVI (1941), 1007–19.

Bb265 . . . , 'Ronsard and Du B. on their Pindaric collaboration', *Rom. Rev.*, XXXIII (1942), 3–25.

Bb266 . . . , 'Du B. and Hellenic Poetry', *PMLA*, LX (1945), 66–80, 356–63, 670–81, 949–58.

Bb267 Six, André, 'Explication française: Du B. *Antiquitez de Rome*, sonnet III', *Romance Notes*, VIII (1966–7), 281–4.

Bb268 Spenser, Edmund, 'The visions of Bellay', in *Muiopotmos*, London, 1590.*

Bb269 . . . , 'Ruines of Rome', in *Prosopopia*, London, 1591.

Bb270 Spitzer, Leo, 'The Poetic Treatment of a Platonic-Christian Theme. [Du B.'s sonnet of the Idea]', *Comp. Lit.*, VI (1954), 193–217. Also in *Romanische Literaturstudien 1936–1956*, Tübingen: Max Niemeyer, 1959, pp. 130–59.

Bb271 Stanford, Will. B., 'On Some References to Ulysses in French Literature from Du B. to Fénélon', *SP*, L (1953), 446–56.

Bb272 ..., 'Attitudes towards Ulysses in French Literature from Du B. to Fénélon', appendix to *The Ulysses Theme. A Study of the Adaptability of a Traditional Hero*, Oxford: Basil Blackwell, 1963, pp. 304–12.

Bb273 Steiner, Arpad, 'Glosses on Du B. – 1. "Heureux qui comme Ulysse", 2. Du B.'s conception of the ideal poet', *MP*, XXIV (1926–7), 167–71.

Bb274 Stemplinger, Eduard, 'Du B. und Horaz', *Archiv*, CXII (1904), 80–93.

Bb275 Tielrooy, J. B., 'De celle qui fut Olive', *Neophilologus*, I (1916), 18–22.

Bb276 Trencsenyi-Waldapfel, Imre, 'Le Symbole d'Ulysse chez Cicéron et J. Du B.', *BGB* (1959), 522–6.* Also résumé in *Ass. G. Budé*, Congrès de Lyon (8–13 Sept. 1958), Paris: Les Belles Lettres, 1960, pp. 376–7.
.1 McFarlane, I. D., *YWMLS*, XXII (1960), 70.
.2 Sozzi, L., *St. fr.*, X (1960), 134.

Bb277 Turquety, Edouard, 'Poëtes françois du seizième siècle, J. Du B., 1560', *BBB*, série 16 (Nov. 1864), 1125–59.

Bb278 Utenhove, Charles, 'Tumulus [for Du B.]', in *Epitaphium in mortem Henrici Gallorum regis christianissimi ejus nominis secundi*, Paris: Robert Estienne, 1560.* See also Ba36.

Bb279 Vaganay, Hugues, 'J. Du B. et les *Rime diverse di molti eccellentissimi autori*', *RHLF*, VIII (1901), 687.

Bb280 ..., 'Du nouveau sur Du B.', *BBB*, n.s. 8 (1929), 268–9.

Bb281 Van Bever, Adolphe, 'Bibliographie de J. Du B.', *RR*, XIII, 12ᵉ année (July–Sept. 1912), 176–88; (Oct.–Dec. 1912), 240–4.

Van der Noot, Jan: see Noot, Jan van der

Bb282 Vanuxem, Paul F., 'Un Normand volé: Vauquelin de la Fresnaye (dont un sonnet serait la source du sonnet de Du B.: "Heureux qui comme Ulysse ... ")', *Le Pays d'Argentan* (Mar. 1932), * (Revue trimestrielle du Syndicat d'Initiative).
.1 Plattard, J., *RSS*, XIX (1932–3), 146–7.

Bb283 Vianey, Joseph, 'Les *Antiquitez de Rome,* leurs sources latines et italiennes', *Bull. it.,* I (1901), 187–99. See Ba69.

Bb284 . . . , 'Le Sonnet LXXXIV de l'*Olive*', *RHLF,* VIII (1901), 323–4.

Bb285 . . . , 'La Part de l'imitation dans les *Regrets*', *Bull. it.,* IV (1904), 30–48.

Bb286 Viatte, M., 'Du B. et les démionaques', *RHLF,* LI (1951), 456–60.
.1 England, S. L., *YWMLS,* XIII (1951), 36.

Bb287 Vipper, Ju., 'Du B. et les voies de développement de la poésie française', *Voprosy literatury.* The reference given in Ae21 appears to be incorrect, and it has not so far been possible to trace this article.

Bb288 . . . , 'La Poésie de Du B. et sa portée historique', *BRP,* II (1963), 77–95.

Bb289 Virolle, R., 'Commentaires de textes I. Quelques "lettres" de Du B. à Ronsard', *L'Ecole,* XLVII, 3 (29.10.55), 93–5.*

Bb290 Vladislav, Jan, [Foreword] in *Du B. Stesky. Z francouzštiny přeložil a poznámkámi opatril Edgar Knobloch, Předmluvu napsal Jan Vladislav,* Prague: Státní nakl. krásné lit-ry a umění, 1964.* (Works. From the French translated and annotated by E. K. Foreword by J. V.)

Bb291 Ward, H. G., 'Du B. and Shakespeare', *Notes and Queries,* 155 (1928), 417.

Bb292 . . . , 'J. Du B. and Sir Thomas Browne', *Review of English Studies,* V (1929), 59–60.

Bb293 Weinberg, Bernard, 'Du B.'s *Contre les Pétrarquistes*', *EC,* XII, 3 (1972), 159–77.

Bb294 Wells, Margaret B.[née Brady], 'Du B.'s sonnet sequence *Songe*', *FS,* XXVI (1972), 1–8.
.1 Wilson, D. B., *St. fr.,* XLVIII (1972), 452.

Bb294a . . . , 'Du B. and Fracastoro', *MLR,* LXVIII (1973), 756–61.

Bb295 Whitney, Mark S., 'Du B. in April 1549, Continuum and Change', *FR,* XLIV, (1970–1), 852–61.
.1 Sharratt, P., *YWMLS,* XXXIII (1971), 91–2.

Bb296 Wierenga, L., '*Les Regrets,* de Du B. Satire et Elégie? A propos de l'édition M. A. Screech des *Regrets*', *Neophilologus,* LVII (1973), 144–55.

Bb297 Wiley, William L., 'Du B. and Ovid', *Romance Notes,* VIII (1966–7), 98–104.

Bb298 Wilmotte, Maurice, 'La Tradition didactique du moyen âge chez J. Du B.', in *Etudes critiques sur la tradition littéraire en France,* Paris: Champion, 1909, pp. 179–200. See also *Revue de l'instruction publique en Belgique,* XLVIII (1905), 81–95.*

Bb299 Wittschier, H. W., 'Du B.', in *Dichtungslehren der Romania aus der Zeit der Renaissance und des Barock.* Hrsg. u. eingeleitet von August Buck, Kl. Heitmann und Walter Mettmann (Ffm: Athenäum 1972), pp. 17–63 (Dokumente zur europäischen Poetik, 3).

Bb300 Young, Douglas, 'Du B. in Fife' [Paraphrase of *Regrets* 31], in *A Braird o Thistles,* Glasgow: W. Maclellan, 1947, p. 15.

Bb301 Z., 'J. Du B. et le Palais Farnèse', *Journal des Débats* (21.5.21).*

THESES ON SIXTEENTH-CENTURY LITERATURE
which judging from the abstracts, when available,
are likely to be of interest

* * *

Bc1 Adamany, Richard G., 'Daniel's debt to foreign literature and *Delia* edited', Ph.D. thesis, Univ. of Wisconsin, 1963. *DA*, XXIII (1963), 4350–1.

Bc2 Asher, R. E., 'The Attitude of French Writers of the Renaissance to early French History, with special reference to their treatment of the Trojan legend and to the influence of Annius of Viterbo', Ph.D. thesis, University College, London, 1955.

Bc3 Atkinson, James B., 'Naiveté and French Renaissance Poetics', Ph.D. thesis, Columbia Univ., 1968. *DA*, XXXII (1971), 378-A.

Bc4 Azibert, Mireille M.-L., 'L'Influence d'Horace et de Cicéron sur les arts de rhétorique première et seconde sur les arts poétiques du seizième siècle en France', Ph.D. thesis, Univ. of Pennsylvania, 1969. *DA*, XXX (1970), 4975-A–6-A.

Bc5 Bannerman, Edith I., 'Les Influences françaises en Ecosse au temps de Marie Stuart', Doctoral thesis, Univ. of Besançon, 1929.

Bc6 Banta, Josephine D., 'Salmon Macrin (1490–1557) and his circle as revealed in his works', Ph.D. thesis, Univ. of Michigan, 1941.

Bc7 Bishop, Robert K., 'The Theme of Death in French Literature from Villon's *Grand Testament* to the middle of the 16th century', Ph.D. thesis, Princeton Univ., 1943.

Bc8 Bolgar, Robert R., 'The Development of Hellenism during the fifteenth and sixteenth centuries', Ph.D. thesis, King's College, Cambridge, 1939–40.

Bc9 Boyd, Theodora R., 'The art of composition of Olivier de Magny', Ph.D. thesis, Radcliffe College, 1943.

Bc10 Braunrot, Bruno, 'L'Imagination poétique chez Du Bartas: Eléments de sensibilité baroque dans la *Création du monde*', Ph.D. thesis, Yale Univ., 1970. *DA*, XXXI (1970), 2906-A.

Bc11 Brosilow, Rosalie, 'Petrarchism in Agrippa d'Aubigné's *L'Hecatombe à Diane*', Ph.D. thesis, Case Western Reserve Univ., 1970. *DA,* XXXI (1970), 3540-A.

Bc12 Brown, Clarence A., 'The Platonic doctrine of inspiration and the nature and function of poetry in Renaissance literary criticism', Ph.D. thesis, Univ. of Wisconsin, 1941.

Bc13 Castor, Grahame D., 'The Terminology of Pléiade Poetics', Ph.D. thesis, Gonville and Caius College, Cambridge, 1961–2. See Bd31.

Bc14 Church, Jo Ann N., 'Satirical Elements in the works of Agrippa d'Aubigné', Ph.D. thesis, Univ. of Wisconsin, 1971. *DA,* XXXI (1970), 6544-A.

Bc15 Clark, J. E., 'The *élégie* in French Literature of the sixteenth century', D.Phil. thesis, Queen's College, Oxford, 1962.

Bc16 Clements, Robert J., 'Critical Opinions of the Pléiade expressed in their poetic works', Ph.D. thesis, Univ. of Chicago, 1940. See also Bd42.

Bc17 Cooper, M. A., 'A Study of sixteenth-century translations of Virgil into French', M.A. thesis, Univ. of Leeds, 1961.

Bc18 Coulter, Mary W., 'The Genre of Satire in French Literature of the Sixteenth Century from 1530–85', Ph.D. thesis, Univ. of S. California, 1953. *Univ. of S. California Abstracts of theses,* 1953, 50–2.

Bc19 Crosby, Virginia, 'Agrippa d'Aubigné's *Les Tragiques*: The Conquest of Profaned Time', Ph.D. thesis, Univ. of S. California, 1969. *DA,* XXX (1970), 5404-A–5-A.

Bc20 Daemmrich, Ingrid G., 'The Ruins motif in French Literature', Ph.D. thesis, Wayne State Univ., 1970. *DA,* XXXI (1970), 3499-A.

Bc21 Daley, Tatham A., 'Jean de la Taille (1533–1608). Etude historique et littéraire', Doctoral thesis, Univ. of Paris, 1934.

Bc22 Davis, Joan H., 'L'Elégie ronsardienne', Ph.D. thesis, Univ. of Texas, 1966. *DA,* XXVII (1967), 2148-A–9-A.

Bc23 Erkelenz, H., 'Ronsard und seine Schule. Eine literarhistorische Studie, als Beitrag zur französische Literaturgeschichte des XVI Jahrhunderts', Ph.D. thesis, Univ. of Jena, 1868.

Bc24 Finn, Sister Dorothy M., 'Love and Marriage in Renaissance Literature', Ph.D. thesis, Columbia Univ., 1955. DA, XV (1955), 2188–9.

Bc25 Forster, Elborg (née Hamacher), 'Die französische Elegie im 16. Jahrhundert', Ph.D. thesis, Univ. of Cologne, 1959.

Bc26   Fortescue, C. R., 'Classical Mythology in French Sixteenth-Century Poetry, with special reference to the works of Ronsard', B.Litt. thesis, St. Hugh's College, Oxford, 1956–7.

Bc27   Francis, K. H., 'The Decline of Chivalry as shown in the French Literature of the XVIth century, with special reference to poetry and drama', Ph.D. thesis, Univ. of London (External), 1948.

Bc28   Freeman, John F., 'French Humanists and politics under Francis I', Ph.D. thesis, Univ. of Michigan, 1969. *DA*, XXX (1969), 1945-A–6-A.

Bc29   Freitag, Günter, 'Studien zu den Epitaphes und Complaintes in der französischen Literatur der Renaissance', Ph.D. thesis, Univ. of Marburg, 1952.

Bc30   Garaud, Christian, 'Le Thème des ruines dans la littérature latine', Thèse de 3e cycle, Univ. of Poitiers, 1961.

Bc31   Ghigo, Francis, 'The Vocabulary of Mellin de Saint-Gelays', Ph.D. thesis, Univ. of N. Carolina, 1943.

Bc32   Götz, Edith E., 'Französische Vergil-Ubersetzungen des 16. Jahrhunderts', Ph.D. thesis, Univ. of Freiburg, 1958.

Bc33   Greene, Thomas M., 'The Epithalamion in the Renaissance', Ph.D. thesis, Yale Univ., 1955.

Bc34   Guggenheim, Josef, 'Quellenstudien zu Samuel Daniel's Sonettencyklus *Delia*', Ph.D. thesis, Univ. of Berlin, 1898.

Bc35   Hallowell, Robert E., 'The Fortune of the Roman Elegists, Propertius and Tibullus, in 16th-century France, with special reference to Ronsard', Ph.D. thesis, Univ. of Illinois, 1942. See Bd97.

Bc36   Harmer, Lewis C., 'The Life and Works of Lancelot de Carle', Ph.D. thesis, Fitzwilliam House, Cambridge, 1936–7.

Bc37   Henningsen, Wilhelm,'Das Verhältnis der französischen Plejadendichtung zur älteren französischen Literatur', Ph.D. thesis, Univ. of Kiel, 1914.

Bc38   Hester, Ralph M., 'Pierre Poupo, an unknown 16th-century poet', Ph.D. thesis, Univ. of California, L.A., 1963. *DA*, XXIV (1964), 3336–7. See Bd105.

Bc39   Hofmannsthal, Hugo H. E. von, 'Ueber den Sprachgebrauch bei den Dichtern der Plejade', Ph.D. thesis, Univ. of Vienna, 1898.

Bc40   Jack, Ronald D. S., 'The Scottish Sonnet and Renaissance Poetry', Ph.D. thesis, Univ. of Edinburgh, 1967–8.

Bc41   Jenkins, Howell, 'Les Bienséances dans la tragédie française de la Renaissance', Doctoral thesis, Univ. of Paris, 1957.

Bc42   Kalwies, Howard H., 'Hugues Salel: a study of his life and works', Ph.D. thesis, Univ. of Kentucky, 1969. *DA*, XXX (1970), 3431-A.

Bc43   Kaun, Ernst, 'Konventionelles in den Elizabethanischen Sonetten mit Berücksichtigung der französischen und italienischen Quellen', Ph.D. thesis, Univ. of Griefswald, 1915.

Bc44   Kell, Barbara, 'Die Bedeutung des Wortes "gloire" bei der Plejade', Ph.D. thesis, Univ. of Würzburg, 1947.

Bc45   Kerr, William A. R., 'Platonic love theories in the Renaissance, with special regard to France', Ph.D. thesis, Harvard Univ., 1904.

Bc46   Kretschmer, Francis A., 'The *Satyres Françoises* of Vauquelin de la Fresnaye', Ph.D. thesis, New York Univ., 1971. *DA*, XXXII (1972), 5795-A.

Bc47   Lapp, John C., 'The New World in French Poetry of the Renaissance', Ph.D. thesis, Cornell Univ., 1943.

Bc48   Larwill, Paul H., 'La Théorie de la traduction au début de la Renaissance. D'après les traductions imprimées en France entre 1477 et 1527', Ph.D. thesis, Univ. of Munich, 1934.

Bc49   Lemeland, Charles A., 'Agrippa d'Aubigné, polémiste', Doctoral thesis, Univ. of Paris, 1961.

Bc50   Levtow, Harry, 'The Convention of Revolt: Origins of the Renaissance Realistic Lyric', Ph.D. thesis, Columbia Univ., 1958. *DA*, XIX (1959), 2338–9.

Bc51   Litchfield, Florence L., 'The Treatment of the Theme of Mutability in the Literature of the English Renaissance: A Study of the Problem of Change between 1558 and 1660', Ph.D. thesis, Univ. of Minnesota, 1935.

Bc52   Lucius, Henriette, 'La Littérature "visionnaire" en France du début du XVIe au début du XIXe siècle. Etude de sémantique et de littérature', Ph.D. thesis, Univ. of Basel, 1970.

Bc53   Lyons, J. C., 'The Poetic Theory of Obscurity in French Literature of the Sixteenth Century', Ph.D. thesis, Univ. of N. Carolina, 1927.

Bc54   Mackay, Alistair R., 'Olivier de Magny: an analysis of his work and its relationship to that of the Pléiade', Ph.D. thesis, Univ. of California Berkeley, 1964. *DA*, XXV(1964), 1917–8.

Bc55   Maddison, Carol H., 'Apollo and the Nine: the Renaissance-baroque ode in Italy, France and England', Ph.D. thesis, Johns Hopkins Univ., 1956–7. See Bd144.

Bc56   Mallet, B. J., 'The nature and function of the imagery in Ronsard's love poetry, with special reference to the sonnet collections', D.Phil. thesis, Exeter College, Oxford, 1970.

Bc57   Matzke, Josef, 'Ronsard's Anfänge', Ph.D. thesis, Univ. of Vienna, 1908.

Bc58   Mayer, C. A., 'Satire in French Literature from 1525 to 1560 with particular reference to the source and the technique', Ph.D. thesis, University College, London, 1949.

Bc59   McCown, Gary M., 'The Epithalamium in the English Renaissance', Ph.D. thesis, Univ. of N. Carolina, Chapel Hill, 1968. *DA,* XXIX (1969),2220-A–1-A.

Bc60   Metcalf, Reginald, 'A Study of French word-order in the sixteenth century with special reference to inversion of the subject', M.A. thesis, Univ. of Leeds, 1949.

Bc61   Meyer, Ernst, 'Studier i den Ronsardska skolans poesi', Ph.D. thesis, Univ. of Uppsala, 1883.

Bc62   Michel, Julian G., 'Horace and the *Odes* of Ronsard: A study of imitation', Ph.D. thesis, Tulane University, 1954.

Bc63   Miller, Elinor S., 'Rhetorical structure in selected works of Ronsard', Ph.D. thesis, Univ. of Chicago, 1966–7.

Bc64   Morrison, Mary G., 'The Influence of Catullus in the sixteenth century in France', Ph.D. thesis, Newnham College, Cambridge, 1940.

Bc65   Müller, Alwin, 'Weckherlin und die Plejade', Ph.D. thesis, Univ. of Munich, 1925.

Bc66   Nelson, John C., 'Giordano Bruno's *Eroici furori* and Renaissance Love Theory', Ph.D. thesis, Columbia Univ., 1954. *DA,* XV (1955), 270–1.

Bc67   Nichols, Fred J., 'The Literary Relationships of the *Poemata* of Julius Caesar Scaliger', Ph.D. thesis, New York Univ., 1967. *DA,* XXVIII (1968), 4641-A.

Bc68   Osborn, Albert W., 'Sir Philip Sidney en France', Doctoral thesis, Univ. of Paris, 1932.

Bc69   Porter, A. H., 'The Satirical Eulogy in the Literature of the French Renaissance', Ph.D. thesis, Bedford College, London, 1966.

Bc70   Preston, Arline F., 'Primitivism in French Literature of the
        sixteenth century', Ph.D. thesis, Johns Hopkins Univ., 1951.

Bc71   Primer, Blossom R., 'Philippe Desportes: a study in late
        Petrarchan style', Ph.D. thesis, Columbia Univ., 1964. *DA,*
        XXVIII (1967), 1083-A–4-A.

Bc72   Radoff, M. L., 'Two Mediaevalists in the French Renaissance;
        Claude Fauchet and Etienne Pasquier', M.A. thesis, Univ. of
        N. Carolina, 1927.

Bc73   Rees, Compton, 'The Hercules Myth in Renaissance poetry
        and prose', Ph.D. thesis, Rice University, 1961–2.

Bc74   Riniker, Rudolf, 'Die Preziosität in der französische
        Renaissancepoesie', Ph.D. thesis, Univ. of Zurich, 1898.

Bc75   Seiler, Mary H., 'Anne de Marquets. Poétesse religieuse du
        XVIe siècle', Ph.D. thesis, Catholic Univ. of America,
        1931. (Also published Washington, 1931).

Bc76   Shipman, George R., 'Louis Meigret (fl. 1550)', Ph.D.
        thesis, Yale Univ., 1950.

Bc77   Siepmann, Helmut, 'Die allegorische Tradition im Werke
        Clement Marots', Inaugural Dissertation, Univ. of Bonn,
        1968.
        .1 Giraud, Y., *BHR,* XXXI (1969), 391–5.

Bc78   Silvestrini, Angelo G., 'L'Arétin et la France au XVIe siècle',
        Ph.D. thesis, Yale Univ., 1956–7.

Bc79   Simpson, Lurline V., 'Borrowings of the Pléiade from
        Classical and Medieval Didactic Treatises', Ph.D. thesis,
        Univ. of Washington, 1928.

Bc80   Stone, Donald, 'The Platonic Ladder – the function of love
        in Ronsard's poetic creation', Ph.D. thesis, Yale Univ.,
        1962–3.

Bc81   Taylor, Mary E., 'The Influence of Platonism on certain
        French authors of the sixteenth century', M. Litt. thesis,
        Girton College, Cambridge, 1930.

Bc82   Terrill, Carol J., 'The Pléiade and the school of Fontainebleau',
        M.A. thesis, Univ. of Kansas, 1957.

Bc83   Terry, Barbara A., 'The Life and Works of Jean-Antoine de
        Baïf', Ph.D. thesis, Univ. of Alabama, 1966. *DA,* XXVII
        (1966), 1354-A.

Bc84   Thomas, D. H., 'The theme of the seasons in sixteenth-
        century French poetry 1550–1580', M.A. thesis, Univ. of
        Bristol, 1965–6.

Bc85   Thomas, Gwenda, 'Les Elégiaques latins en France au XVIe siècle', Doctoral thesis, Univ. of Paris, 1951.

Bc86   Ungerer, Dieter, 'Das Dichterideal der Plejade', Ph.D. thesis, Univ. of Tübingen, 1961.

Bc87   Voigt, Arno, 'Das dichterische Selbstgefühl bei den französischen Dichtern des 16. und 17. Jahrhunderts', Ph.D. thesis, Univ. of Jena, 1922.

Bc88   Voigt, Julius, 'Das Naturgefühl in der Literatur der französische Renaissance', Ph.D. thesis, Univ. of Berlin, 1898.

Bc89   Voigt, Kurt, 'Estienne Pasquier's Stellung zur Pléiade', Ph.D. thesis, Univ. of Leipzig, 1902.

Bc90   Weiner, Ludwig, 'Das Deminutivum in der Zeit der Plejade', Ph.D. thesis, Univ. of Vienna, 1914.

Bc91   Welsh, Susan M., 'The Art of Pierre de Ronsard's Sonnets', Ph.D. thesis, Yale Univ., 1963—4.

Bc92   Wien, Ludwika, 'Der Todesgedanke in der französischen Dichtung der Renaissance', Ph.D. thesis, Univ. of Vienna, 1936.

Bc93   Wilcox, Alfred M., 'Antoine de Montchrestien: *La Bergerie, A Critical Edition*', Ph.D. thesis, Univ. of Pennsylvania, 1959. *DA*, XX (1959), 2306.

Bc94   Wildermann, H., 'Catull bei den Dichtern der Plejade', Ph.D. thesis, Univ. of Tübingen, 1949.

Bc95   Wilson, Dudley B., 'La Poésie champêtre chez Pierre de Ronsard', Doctoral thesis, Univ. of Paris, 1953.

Bc96   Wyatt, J. M., 'Indépendance et servilité chez un poète de cour, Ronsard', M.A. thesis, Univ. of Exeter, 1970.

*

For theses published under their original titles see:

Ba10, 15, 20, 31, 35, 46, 48, 51, 61, 73

Bb15

Bd6, 11, 13, 14, 15, 28, 29, 32, 40, 41, 50, 59, 63, 69, 70, 77, 80, 84, 86, 94, 99, 101, 102, 111, 113, 115, 117, 120, 121, 122, 126, 128, 129, 139, 148, 157, 171, 181, 183, 189, 191, 200, 201, 202, 208, 220, 224, 240

BOOKS IN WHICH SIGNIFICANT REFERENCE IS MADE TO DU BELLAY

* * *

Bd1   Addamanio, Natale, *Il Rinascimento in Francia. Pietro Ronsard (1524–1585)*, Palermo: Saggio di letteratura comparata, Rome: Remo Sandron, 1925.
.1   Jourda, P., *RLC*, X (1930), 801–3.
.2   ... , *RSS*, XIII (1926), 143–7.
.3   Tanquerey, F. J., *YWMLS*, I (1931), 48.

Bd2   Alter, Jean, V., *Les Origines de la satire anti-bourgeoise en France. Moyen Age. XVIe siècle*, Geneva: Droz, 1966. See Be61.
.1   Bowen, B. C., *MLR*, LXIV (1969), 163–5.
.2   Crow, J., *FS*, XXIII (1969), 54–6.
.3   McFarlane, I. D., *YWMLS*, XXVIII (1966), 58.

Bd3   Armstrong, Elizabeth, *Ronsard and the Age of Gold*, Cambridge UP, 1968.
.1   Castor, G., *FS*, XXIV (1970), 51–2.
.2   Giraud, Y., *BHR*, XXXI (1969), 399–401.
.3   Joukovsky, F., *RHLF*, LXIX (1969), 1026–7.
.4   Richter, M., *St. fr.*, XXXVIII (1969), 334.
.5   Stone, D., *MLR*, LXIV (1969), 668–9.
.6   Wilson, D. B., *YWMLS*, XXX (1968), 73.

Bd4   *Art littéraire et préludes au grand siècle*, Paris: Les Classiques Quillet, 1954. *
.1   England, S. L., *YWMLS*, XVI (1954), 54.

Bd5   Aubertin, Charles, *La Versification française et ses nouveaux théoriciens. Les règles classiques et les libertés modernes*, Paris: Belin frères, 1898.

Bd6   Augé-Chiquet, Mathieu, *La Vie, les idées et l'œuvre de Jean-Antoine de Baïf*, Paris: Hachette; Toulouse: Privat, 1909. Doctoral thesis, Univ. of Paris, 1909–10.
.1   Vianey, J., *RHLF*, XVIII (1911), 204–9.

Bd7   Babelon, Jean, *La Civilisation française de la Renaissance*, Tournai: Casterman, 1961.
.1   Sozzi, L., *St. fr.*, XVII (1962), 330.

Bd8   Bailbé, Jacques, *Agrippa d'Aubigné – poète des "Tragiques"*, Univ. de Caen, 1968.
.1 Hall, K. M., *FS*, XXIV (1970), 168–70.
.2 Pineaux, J., *RHLF*, LXX (1970), 120–1.
.3 Regosin, R., *Rom. Rev.*, LXIII (1972), 45–7.

Bd9   Baldwin, Charles S., *Renaissance Literary Theory and Practice. Classicism in the Rhetoric and Poetry of Italy, France and England*, New York: Columbia UP, 1939.
.1 Atkins, J. W. H., *MLR*, XXXVI (1941), 522–4.

Bd10   Balmas, Enea, *Un poeta del Rinascimento francese, Etienne Jodelle: la sua vita, il suo tempo*, Firenze (Biblioteca dell' *Archivum Romanicum*, série I, vol. 66), 1962.
.1 Lebègue, R., *RHLF*, LXIV (1964), 669–70.
.2 McFarlane, I. D., *YWMLS*, XXIV (1962), 82.
.3 Richter, M., *St. fr.*, XXVI (1965), 297–9.

Bd11   Banašević, Nicolas, *Jean Bastier de la Péruse (1529–1554), étude biographique et littéraire*, Paris: Presses Universitaires de France, 1923. Doctoral thesis, Univ. of Paris, 1923–4.

Bd12   Baur, Albert, *Maurice Scève et la renaissance lyonnaise: Etude d'histoire littéraire*, Paris: Champion, 1906.

Bd13   Becker, Abraham H., *Un Humaniste au XVIe siècle. Loys Le Roy (Ludovicus Regius) de Coutances*, Paris: Oudin, 1896. Doctoral thesis, Univ. of Paris, 1896–7.
.1 Delaruelle, L., *RHLF*, IV (1897), 614–9.

Bd14   Becker, Karl, *Syntaktische Studien über die Plejade*, Darmstadt, 1885. * Doctoral thesis, Univ. of Leipzig, 1885–6.

Bd15   Berger, Bruno, *Vers rapportés. Ein Beitrag zur Stilgeschichte der französischen Renaissancedichtung*, Freiburg, 1930.* Doctoral thesis, Univ. of Karlsruhe, 1930.

Bd16   Bergounioux, Louis A., *Un Précurseur de la Pléiade: Hugues Salel de Cazals-en-Quercy (1504–1553)*, Paris & Toulouse: Guitard, 1930.
.1 Jourda, P., *RHLF*, XXXVII (1930), 610–11.
.2 Tanquerey, F. J., *YWMLS*, II (1932), 40.

Bd17   Bertrand, Anthoine de, *Troisième livre de chansons*, Paris: Roy & Ballard, 1578. Also ed. H. Expert, Paris: Senart, 1927. See Bb17, Be250.

Bd18   Bienaimé, Dora R., *Grévin poeta satirico e altri saggi sulla poesia del Cinquecento Francese*, Pisa: Giardini, 1967.*
.1 Cameron, K., *BHR*, XXXI (1969), 388–9.
.2 Logan, M. R., *RHLF*, LXX (1970), 697–8.

Bd19 Binet, Claude, *La Vie de Pierre de Ronsard de Claude Binet, 1586,* édn critique avec introduction et commentaire historique et critique par Paul Laumonier, Paris: Hachette, 1901, 1910 (also Geneva: Slatkine Reprints, 1969).
.1 Chamard H., *RHLF,* XVII (1910), 634–42.
.2 Tilley, A., *MLR,* VI (1911), 268–71.

Bd20 Bishop, Morris G., *Ronsard, Prince of Poets,* London: Oxford UP, 1940.
.1 David, J., *MLQ,* II (1941), 339.
.2 Lawton, H. W., *MLR,* XXXVI (1941), 269.
.3 Nitze, W. A., *MLN,* LVI (1941), 231–2.

Bd21 Blignières, Auguste de, *Essai sur Amyot et les traducteurs français au XVIᵉ siècle,* Paris: Durand, 1851.
.1 Marty-Laveaux, C., *Bibliothèque de l'Ecole des Chartes,* 3ᵉ série, III (1851), 497.*

Boase, Alan: see Bd93.

Bd22 Bonnot, Jacques, *Humanisme et Pléiade. L'Histoire, la doctrine, les œuvres,* Paris: Hachette, 1959.

Bd23 Bourciez, Edouard, *Les Mœurs polies et la littérature de cour sous Henri II,* Paris: Hachette, 1886. Also Geneva: Slatkine reprints, 1967.

Bd24 Bowen, Barbara C. [née Cannings], *Les Caractéristiques essentielles de la farce française et leur survivance dans les années 1550–1620,* Urbana: Illinois Studies in Language and Literature, 53, 1964. See Be29.
.1 Frappier, J., *Rom. Phil.* XIX (1965–6), 637–41.
.2 Garapon, R., *RHLF,* LXV (1965), 696–7.
.3 Lehnberger, S., *MLN,* LXXX (1965), 648–9.
.4 Lewicka, H., *ZRP,* III–IV (1966), 400–5.
.5 McFarlane, I. D., *YWMLS,* XXVI (1964), 70.

Bd25 Brunetière, Ferdinand, *L'Evolution des genres dans l'histoire de la littérature,* Paris: Hachette, 1890.

Bd26 ..., *Histoire de la littérature française classique 1515–1830 (–1875),* Paris: Delagrave, 1904–17.
.1 Séché, L., *RR,* VI, 5ᵉ année (Mar.–Apr. 1905), 115–9.

Bd27 Buck, August, *Zu Begriff und Probleme der Renaissance,* Darmstadt: Wissenschaftliche Buchgesellschaft, 1969.
.1 Schalk, F., *Arcadia,* VI (1971), 200–3.

Bd28 Busson, Henri, *Dans l'orbe de la Pléiade: Charles d'Espinay, évêque de Dol, poète (1531? –1591),* Paris: Champion, 1922. Thèse complémentaire, Univ. of Paris, 1922–3.

Bd29 . . . , *Les Sources et le développement du rationalisme dans
la littérature de la Renaissance (1533–1601)*, Paris: Letouzey
et Ané, Rennes: Oberthür, 1922, Paris: Vrin, 1957. Doctoral
thesis, Univ. of Paris, 1922–3.
.1 Müller, A., 'Chronique littéraire du XVIe siècle',
L'Enseignement chrétien (Mar. 1958).*
.2 Renaudet, A., *RHLF,* XXXI (1924), 536–46.
.3 Tanquerey, F. J., *YWMLS,* II (1932), 40.

Bd30 Cameron, Alice, *Influence of Ariosto's epic and lyric poetry
on Ronsard and his group,* Baltimore: Johns Hopkins Press,
1930.
.1 Champion, E., *RLC,* X (1930), 588.
.2 Fucilla, J. G., *Giornale storico della letteratura italiana,*
CI (1933), 145–7.
.3 Jerrold, M. F., *MLR,* XXVI (1931), 500–1.
.4 Jourda, P., *Revue critique,* XCVII (1930), 328–9.
.5 Merrill, R. V., *MP,* XXVIII (1930–1), 378–9.
.6 Tanquerey, F. J., *YWMLS,* II (1932), 40.
.7 Vianey, J., *MLN,* XLVI (1931), 126–9.

Bd31 Castor, Grahame D., *Pléiade Poetics. A Study in 16th-
Century Thought and Terminology,* Cambridge UP, 1964.
See also Bc13.
.1 Armstrong, E., *MLR,* LXI (1966), 130–1.
.2 Lawton, H. W., *FS,* XIX (1965), 179–80.
.3 McFarlane, I. D., *YWMLS,* XXVI (1964), 67.
.4 Richter, M., *St. fr.,* XXV (1965), 139.
.5 Weber, H., *RHLF,* LXVI (1966), 499–50.

Bd32 Cave, Terence C., *Devotional Poetry in France, c. 1570–
1613,* Cambridge UP, 1969. Doctoral thesis, Univ. of
Cambridge 1965–66.
.1 Higman, F., *MLR,* LXV (1970), 419–20.
.1 Pineaux, J., *RHLF,* LXX (1970), 699.
.3 Richter, M., *St. fr.,* XL (1970), 112–4.
.4 Wilson, D. B., *FS,* XXIV (1970), 395–6.
.5 . . . , *YWMLS,* XXX (1968), 75.

Bd33 Cecchetti, Dario, *Il Petrarchismo in Francia,* Turin:
G. Giappichelli, 1970.

Bd34 Chamard, Henri, *Les Origines de la poésie française de la
Renaissance,* Paris: Fontemoing, 1920.
.1 Anon., *RLC,* I (1921), 322–3.
.2 Radouant, R., *RHLF,* XXVIII (1921), 593–4.
.3 Tilley, A., *MLR,* XVI (1921), 198–9.

Books in which significant reference is made to Du Bellay

Bd35 ..., *La Doctrine et l'œuvre poétique de la Pléiade* [notes de cours polygraphiées. 10 fasc.], Paris: Grillon, 1931–2.*

Bd36 ..., *Histoire de la Pléiade*, Paris: Didier, 4 vols., 1939–40.
.1 David, J., *MLQ*, I (1940), 121–4.
.2 England, S. L., *YWMLS*, X (1940), 49. (Vols 1 & 2)
.3 ..., *YWMLS*, XI (1941–9), 43. (Vols 3 & 4)
.4 Lebègue, R., *RHLF*, LII (1952), 84–7.
.5 Tanquerey, F. J., *MLR*, XXXV (1940), 552–3. (Vols 1 &2)

Bd37 Champion, Pierre, *Ronsard et son temps*, Paris: Champion, 1925.
.1 Laumonier, P., *RHLF*, XXXV (1928), 111–8.
.2 Tanquerey, F. J., *YWMLS*, I (1931), 47.

Bd38 Charbonnier, Félix, *La Poésie française et les guerres de religion 1560–1574*, Paris: Bureau de la "Revue des Œuvres Nouvelles", 1919. (Cover dated 1920).

Cioccetti, Urbano: see Bd216.

Bd39 Cioranescu, Alexandre I., *L'Arioste en France. Des origines à la fin du XVIIIᵉ siècle*, Paris: Presses modernes, 1939; Turin, 1963.
.1 Beall, C. B., *MLN*, LVII (1942), 234–5.
.2 Lavaud, J., *HR*, VI (1939), 396–8.
.3 McFarlane, I. D., *FS*, XXI (1967), 60–2.
.4 ..., *YWMLS*, XXV (1963), 39.

Bd40 Clément, Louis, *De Adriani Turnebi regii professoris praefationibus et poematis*, Paris: A. Picard, 1899. Thèse complémentaire. Univ. of Paris, 1898–9.

Bd41 ..., *Henri Estienne et son œuvre francaise*, Paris: A. Picard, 1899. Doctoral thesis, Univ. of Paris, 1898–9.
.1 Roy, E., *RHLF*, VII (1900), 144–8.

Bd42 Clements, Robert J., *Critical theory and Practice of the Pléiade*, Cambridge, Mass.: Harvard UP, 1942. See also Bc16.
.1 Carrington Lancaster, H., *MLN*, LVIII (1943), 210–1.
.2 Lawton, H. W., *MLR*, XXXVIII (1943), 157–8.

Bd43 ..., *The Peregrine Muse: Studies in Comparative Renaissance Literature*, Univ. of N. Carolina Studies in Romance Languages and Literatures, 31, Chapel Hill: Univ. of N. Carolina Press, 1959.
.1 Sozzi, L., *St. fr.*, XVII (1962), 329–30.

Bd44 ..., *Picta poesis: literary and humanistic theory in Renaissance emblem books*, Rome: Edizioni di Storia e Letteratura, 1960.

Bd45   Cohen, Gustave, *Ronsard, sa vie et ses œuvres,* Paris: Boivin & cie, 1924. (Also appears as series of articles in *RCC,* 1922 ff.).
.1   Brandin, L., *MLR,* XX (1925), 96–7.
.2   Plattard, J., *RSS,* XI (1924), 330–3.
.3   Raymond, M., *RHLF,* XL (1933), 592–4.
.4   Tanquerey, F. J., *YWMLS,* I (1931), 47.

Bd46   Colletet, Guillaume, *Eloges des hommes illustres . . . composez en latin par Scevole de Sainte-Marthe, et mis en françois par G. Colletet,* Paris, 1644.* See Bb227.

Bd47   . . . , *Art poétique I. Traitté de l'épigramme et traitté du sonnet* (ed. P. A. Jannini), Geneva: T.L.F., 1965.
.1   Castor, G., *FS,* XXI (1967), 240.
.2   Fromilhague, R., *RHLF,* LXVII (1967), 810–2.

Bd48   Darmesteter, Arsène, and Adolphe Hatzfeld, *Le Seizième siècle en France. Tableau de la littérature et de sa langue,* Paris: Delagrave, 1878.
.1   Larroque, Tamizey de, *Polybiblion,* XXII (1878), 334.*
.2   Ulbrich, M., *ZRP* (1879), 289.

Bd49   Dassonville, Michel, *Ronsard: Etude historique et littéraire.* I. – Les Enfances Ronsard, II – A la conquête de la Toison d'Or, Geneva: Droz, 1968, 1970.
.1   Armstrong, E., *MLR,* LXV (1970), 164–6. (Vol I).
.2   Joukovsky, F., *RHLF,* LXXI (1971), 493–4. (Vol I).
.3   Richter, M., *St. fr.,* XXXIX (1969), 534–5. (Vol I).
.4   Wilson, D. B., *YWMLS,* XXX (1968), 73. (Vol I).
.5   . . . , *FS,* XXIV (1970), 284–5. (Vol I).
.6   Hall, K. M., *MLR,* LXVI (1971), 895. (Vol II).
.7   Richter, M., *St. fr.,* XLVI (1972), 139. (Vol II).
.8   Smith, M. C., *BHR,* XXXIII (1971), 722–4. (Vol II).

Bd50   Delacourcelle, Doris, *Le Sentiment de l'art dans la "Bergerie" de Rémy Belleau,* Oxford: Basil Blackwell, 1945. Doctoral thesis, Univ. of Poitiers, 1946.

Bd51   Delcourt, Marie, *Etude sur les traductions des tragiques grecs et latins en France depuis la Renaissance,* Brussels: M. Lamertin, 1925.
.1   Lebègue, R., *RSS,* XIII (1926), 147–50.
.2   Lefranc, A., *Revue historique,* CLIII (1926), 265–6.

Bd52   Delumeau, Jean, *Vie économique et sociale de Rome dans la seconde moitié du XVIe siècle,* Paris: E. de Boccard, 1957–9.

Bd53   . . . , *La Civilisation de la Renaissance,* Paris: Arthaud, 1967.
.1   Lapeyre, H., *BHR,* XXX (1968), 617–22.

Bd54   Delvau, Alfred, *Les Sonneurs de sonnets 1540–1866,* Paris: Librairie Bachelin-Deflorenne, 1867.*

Bd55   Demerson, Guy, *La Mythologie classique dans l'œuvre lyrique de la Pléiade,* Geneva: Droz, 1972.

Bd56   Derche, Roland, *Etudes de textes français,* Paris: Société d'Edition d'Enseignement supérieur, 1965.
       .1 Richter, M., *St. fr.,* XXXII (1967), 331–2.

Bd57   Doucet, Roger, *Les Bibliothèques parisiennes au XVIe siècle,* Paris: J. Picard, 1956.
       .1 Lebègue, R., *RHLF,* LVIII (1958), 533–4.

Bd58   Dreano, Maturin, *La Pléiade. Introduction et notes de M. Dreano,* Angers: J. Petit, 1946.*

       Dresden, Sem: see Bd164.

Bd59   Dubruck, Edelgard, *The Theme of Death in French Poetry of the Middle Ages and the Renaissance,* The Hague: Mouton, 1964. Doctoral thesis, Univ. of Michigan, 1962.
       .1 Graham, V. E., *Rom. Rev.,* LVI (1965), 203–4.
       .2 McFarlane, I. D., *YWMLS,* XXIV (1962), 79. (CR of thesis).

Bd60   Eckhardt, Alexandre, *Rémy Belleau – sa vie, sa "bergerie",* Budapest: Joseph Nemeth, 1917.

Bd61   Egger, Emile, *L'Hellénisme en France,* Paris: Didier, 1869.

Bd62   Elwert, Wilhelm T., *Französische Metrik,* Munich, 1961. Also published as *Traité des versifications françaises des origines à nos jours,* Paris: Klincksieck, 1965.
       .1 Gáldi, L., *BRP,* VI (1967), 391–2. (CR of German version).
       .2 Huber, E., *ZFSP,* LXXII (1962), 230–2.

Bd63   Espiner-Scott, Janet, *Les Sonnets élisabéthains, les sources et l'apport personnel,* Bar-le-Duc: Jolibois, Paris: Champion, 1929. Doctoral thesis, Univ. of Paris, 1929.
       .1 Gourvitch, I., *MLR,* XXV (1930), 345–6.
       .2 Harrison, G. B., *MP,* XXVII (1929–30), 241–2.

Bd64   Faguet, Emile, *Le Seizième siècle, études littéraires,* Paris: Boivin & Cie, 1894.
       .1 Bonnefon, P., *RHLF,* I (1894), 204–6.

Bd65   Favre, Jules, *Olivier de Magny (1529? –1561),* Paris: Garnier, 1885.

Bd66   Febvre, Lucien, *Le Problème de l'incroyance au XVIe siècle. La religion de Rabelais,* Paris: Albin Michel, 1942 and 1968.

Bd67   Festugière, A. M. Jean, *La Philosophie de l'amour de Marcile Ficin et son influence sur la littérature française au XVIᵉ siècle,* Revista da universidade de Coimbra, 1922.* Paris: Etudes de philosophie médiévale, 1941.
        .1 Lavaud, J., *RSS,* XII (1925), 175–7.

Bd68   Fleuret, Fernand, *De Ronsard à Baudelaire,* Paris: Mercure de France, 1935.

Bd69   Fraisse, Simone, *Une conquête du rationalisme. L'influence de Lucrèce en France au XVIᵉ siècle,* Paris: Nizet, 1962. Doctoral thesis, Univ. of Paris, 1961.
        .1 Lebègue, R., *RHLF,* LXIV (1964), 668–9.
        .2 McFarlane, I. D., *YWMLS,* XXV (1963), 39.
        .3 Mombello, G., *St. fr.,* XXI (1963), 505–7.
        .4 Tenenti, A., *Belfagor* (30.ll.63).*

Bd70   Franchet, Henri, *Le Poète et son œuvre d'après Ronsard,* Paris: Champion, 1923. Doctoral thesis, Univ. of Paris, 1922–3.
        .1 Tanquerey, F. J., *YWMLS,* I (1931), 48.

Bd71   Françon, Marcel, *Leçons et notes sur la littérature française du XVIᵉ siècle,* London, Rochecorbon: C. Gay, 1957 (lst edn); Cambridge, Mass.: Schoenhof's foreign books, 1959 [1958] (2nd edn); Cambridge, Mass.: Harvard UP, Oxford UP, 1965 (3rd edn); Cambridge, Mass.: Harvard UP, 1967(4th edn).
        .1 Anon., *FMLS,* II (1966), 288.
        .2 England, S. L., *YWMLS,* XIX (1957), 67.
        .3 Giudici, E., *St. fr.,* V (1958), 269–71.
        .4 Jodogne, P., *St. fr.,* XXXII (1967), 332.
        .5 McFarlane, I. D., *YWMLS,* XXVII (1965), 53.
        .6 . . . , *YWMLS,* XXVIII (1966), 56.
        .7 . . . , *FS,* XXIII (1969), 172–5.

Bd72   Fucilla, Joseph G., *Studies and Notes (Literary and Historical),* Naples: Istituto editoriale del Mezzogiorno, 1953. See Bb92, 93.

Bd73   Gadoffre, Gilbert, *Ronsard par lui-même,* Paris: Seuil, 1960.
        .1 Walker, D. P., *MLR,* LVI (1961), 611–2.

Bd74   Gambier, Henri, *Italie et Renaissance poétique en France. La Renaissance poétique en France au XVIᵉ siècle et l'influence de l'Italie,* Padua: CEDAM, 1936. See Bb95.

Bd75   Gaudin, Paul, *Du Rondeau, du Triolet, du Sonnet,* Paris: Librairie centrale (J. Lemer), 1870.*

Bd76   Gendre, André, *Ronsard, poète de la quête amoureuse,*
        Neuchâtel: La Baconnière, 1970.
        .1 Françon, M., *St. fr.*, XLII (1970), 500—1.
        .2 Smith, M. C., *FS,* XXVI (1972), 321—2.

Bd77   Gerighausen, Josef, *Die historische Deutung der National-*
        sprache im französischen Schriftum des 16. Jahrhunderts,
        Bonn: Romanisches Seminar der Universität, 1963. Doctoral
        thesis, Univ. of Bonn, 1962.
        .1 Kukenheim, L., *Het Franse Boek,* XXXIV (1964), 143—5.
        .2 Leube, E., *Archiv,* CCI (1964), 227—9.
        .3 Prost, W., *St. fr.,* VIII (1964), 531—2.

Bd78   Giraud, Yves F. A., *La Fable de Daphné. Essai sur un type de*
        métamorphose végétale dans la littérature et dans les arts
        jusqu'à la fin du XVIIe siècle, Geneva: Droz, 1969.

Bd79   Giudici, Enzo, *Spiritualismo e carnascialismo.* Aspetti e
        problemi dei cinquecento letterario francese, vol. I, Naples:
        Edizioni scientifiche italiane, 1968.

Bd80   Gordon, Alexander L., *Ronsard et la rhétorique,* Geneva:
        Droz, 1970. Doctoral thesis, Univ. of Paris, 1965.
        .1 Armstrong, E., *MLR,* LXVII (1972), 885—6.
        .2 Tripet, A., *BHR,* XXXV (1973), 157—8.

Bd81   Goukovskaia, Z., *De l'histoire des conceptions linguistiques*
        de la Renaissance, Edns de l'Univ. de Leningrad, 1940.*

Bd82   Graham, Victor E., *Sixteenth-Century French Poetry,*
        Toronto UP, 1964; London: Oxford UP, 1965.
        .1 McFarlane, I. D., *YWMLS,* XXVII (1965), 59.

Bd83   Grant, W. Leonard, *Neo-Latin Literature and the Pastoral,*
        Chapel Hill: Univ. of N. Carolina Press; London: Oxford UP,
        1965.
        .1 McFarlane, I. D., *FMLS,* III (1967), 67—75.

Bd84   Graur, Théodosia, *Un disciple de Ronsard, Amadis Jamyn*
        (1540—1593). Sa vie, son œuvre, son temps, Paris: Champion,
        1929. Doctoral thesis, Univ. of Paris, n.d.
        .1 Jourda, P., *RHLF,* XXXIX (1932), 119—20.
        .2 Tanquerey, F. J., *YWMLS,* I (1931), 48.

Bd85   Grève, Marcel de, *L'Interprétation de Rabelais au XVIe siècle,*
        Geneva: Droz, 1961. (Tome III of *Etudes Rabelaisiennes*).

Bd86   Griffiths, Richard, *The Dramatic Technique of Antoine de*
        Montchrétien, Oxford: Clarendon Press, 1970. Doctoral
        thesis, Univ. of Cambridge, 1962.
        .1 Campagnoli, R., *St. fr.,* XLV (1971), 505—7.

    .2 Hall, K. M., *MLR*, LXVI (1971), 686–7.
    .3 Jondorf, G., *FS*, XXV (1971), 192–3.
    .4 Morel, J., *RHLF*, LXXI (1971), 691.
    .5 Sharratt, P., *YWMLS*, XXXII (1970), 91–2.

Bd87   Grosse, Ernst U., *Sympathie der Natur. Geschichte eines Topos*, Munich: Wilhelm Fink, 1968.

Bd88   Guerrieri Crocetti, Camillo, *G. B. Giraldi e il pensiero critico del secolo XVI*, Milan: Albrighi, Segati & C., 1932.
    .1 Baillou, J., *RLC*, (1934), 598–601.
    .2 Lawton, H. W., *YWMLS*, VI (1935), 52.

Bd89   Gundersheimer, Werner L., *The Life and Works of Louis Le Roy*, Geneva: Droz, 1966.
    .1 Friedman, L. J., *Rom. Phil.*, XXVI (1972), 196–8.
    .2 McFarlane, I. D., *YWMLS*, XXVIII (1966), 57.
    .3 Soulié, M., *RHLF*, LXVIII (1968), 843–4.

Bd90   ... (ed.), *French Humanism 1470–1600*, London: Macmillan, 1969. See Bel5.
    .1 Smith, C. N., *FS*, XXV (1971), 451–2.
    .2 Wilson, D. B., *YWMLS*, XXXI (1969), 72.

Bd91   Guy, Henri, *Réflexions sur un lieu commun*, Bordeaux: Gounouilhon, 1902.*

Bd92   ..., *Histoire de la poésie française au XVIe siècle*, Paris: Champion, 1926. (Vol. II).
    .1 Anon., *RLC*, VI (1926), 693–4.

Bd93   Haggis, D. R. (ed.), *The French Renaissance and its Heritage: Essays presented to Alan Boase*, London: Methuen, 1968. See Be221 and Be249.
    .1 Balmas, E., *RHLF*, LXXI (1971), 692–3.
    .2 Moore, W. G., *MLR*, LXV (1970), 900–1.
    .3 Sayce, R. A., *FS*, XXIII (1969), 324–5.
    .4 Wilson, D. B., *YWMLS*, XXX (1968), 64.

Bd94   Hagiwara, Michio P., *French Epic Poetry in the 16th Century: Theory and Practice*, The Hague, Paris: Mouton, 1972. Doctoral thesis, Univ. of Michigan, 1966. *DA*, XXVII (1967), 3048A–9A.

Bd95   Hall, Kathleen M., *Pontus de Tyard and his "Discours philosophiques"*, Oxford UP, 1963.
    .1 Philips, M. M., *MLR*, LIX (1964), 142.

Bd96   Hall, Vernon, *Renaissance Literary Criticism. A Study of its Social Content*, New York: Columbia UP, 1945.
    .1 Atkins, J. H. W., *MLR*, XLI (1946), 429–30.

Bd97   Hallowell, Robert E., *Ronsard and the Conventional Roman Elegy*, Urbana: Illinois UP, 1954. See Bc35.
.1 Desonay, F., *BHR*, XVII (1955), 123—4.
.2 Hutton, J., *MLN*, LXX (1955), 611—5.

Bd98   Hamon, Auguste, *Un grand rhétoriqueur poitevin: Jean Bouchet (1476—1557)?*, Paris: H. Oudin, 1901. Doctoral thesis, Univ. of Paris, 1900—1.

Bd99   Hartmann, Hans, *Guillaume des Autels (1529—1581?):* *ein französischer Dichter und Humanist*, Zurich: Leeman & Co., 1907. Inaugural Dissertation, Univ. of Zurich, 1907.

Bd100   Hatzfeld, Helmut A., *Die französische Renaissancelyrik*, Munich: M. Hueber, 1924.

Bd101   Hauvette, Henri, *Un exilé florentin à la cour de France au XVIe siècle: Luigi Alamanni (1495—1556); sa vie et son œuvre*, Paris: Hachette, 1903. Doctoral thesis, Univ. of Paris, 1902—3.
.1 Bourciez, E., *Bull. it.*, III (1903), 243—6.
.2 Laumonier, P., *RR*, IV, 3e année (Jan.—Sept., 1903), 258—74. See Be140.

Bd102   Hawkins, Richmond L., *The Life and Works of Maître Charles Fontaine, parisien*, Cambridge, Mass.: Harvard UP, 1916. Doctoral thesis, Harvard Univ., 1908.*
.1 Roy, E., *RHLF*, XXV (1918), 676—9.

Bd103   Hecq, Gaeten M. J. A., and L. Paris, *La Poétique française au moyen âge et à la Renaissance*, Paris: E. Bouillon, Brussels: Société belge de librairie, 1896.

Bd104   Hepp, Noémi, *Homère en France au XVIe siècle*, Turin: Atti della Accademia delle Scienze di Torino (96), 1961—2.*
.1 Marmier, J., *RHLF*, LXIV (1964), 96—7.
.2 McFarlane, I. D., *YWMLS*, XXV (1963), 38—9.

Bd105   Hester, Ralph M., *A Protestant Baroque Poet. Pierre Poupo*, The Hague, Paris: Mouton, 1970. See Bc38.

Bd106   Hope, Thomas E., *Lexical borrowings in the Romance languages: a critical study of Italianisms in French and Gallicisms in Italian from 1100 to 1900*, Oxford: Basil Blackwell, 1971.

Bd107   Hulubei, Alice, *L'Eglogue en France au XVIe siècle. (Epoque des Valois, 1515—89)*, Paris: Droz, 1938.
.1 Lebègue, R., *HR*, VI (1939), 386—8.

Bd108 . . . , *Répertoire des Eglogues en France au XVIe siècle. (Epoque des Valois, 1515–89),*Geneva: Droz, 1939.

Bd109 Hutton, James, *The Greek Anthology in France and in the Latin Writers of the Netherlands to the year 1800,* Ithaca: Cornell UP, 1946.
.1 Lebègue, R., *RHLF,* XLVII (1947), 368–70.
.2 Lytton Sells, A., *MLR,* XLIII (1948), 419–21.

Bd110 Jacobsen, Eric, *Translation, a traditional craft,* Copenhagen: Gyldendalske Boghandel-Nordisk Forlag, 1958.

Jacquot, Jean: see Bb238, Bd162.

Bd111 Janik, Dieter, *Geschichte der Ode und der "Stances" von Ronsard bis Boileau,* Berlin: Gehlen, 1968. Doctoral thesis, Univ. of Tübingen, 1967. See Bb122, 123.
.1 Weber, H., *RHLF,* LXX (1970), 695–7.
.2 Wilson, D. B., *YWMLS,* XXX (1968), 71.

Bd112 Janssen, Willem, *Charles Utenhove, sa vie et son œuvre (1536–1600),* Maastricht, 1939.*
.1 Lebègue, R., *BHR,* II (1942), 217–8.

Bd113 Jasinski, Max, *L'Histoire du sonnet en France,* Douai: Brugère & Dalsheimer, 1903. Doctoral thesis, Univ. of Paris, 1903–4.
.1 Potez, H., *RHLF,* XI (1904), 340–2.

Bd114 Jeanneret, Michel, *Poésie et tradition biblique au XVIe siècle,* Paris: Corti, 1969.

Bd115 Jeffery, Brian, *French Renaissance Comedy 1552–1630,* Oxford: Clarendon Press, 1969. Doctoral thesis, Univ. of St Andrews, 1967–8.
.1 Cameron, K., *BHR,* XXXII (1970), 518–9.
.2 Françon, M., *St. fr.,* XLIII (1971), 133.
.3 Hall, H. G., *MLR,* LXVI (1971), 184–5.
.4 Wilson, D. B., *YWMLS,* XXXI (1969), 85.

Bd116 John, Lisle C., *The Elizabethan Sonnet Sequences. Studies in Conventional Conceits,* New York, Columbia UP, 1938.
.1 Bullough, G., *MLR,* XXXIV (1939), 635–6.

Bd117 Joukovsky, Françoise, *La Gloire dans la poésie française du XVIe siècle. Des Rhétoriqueurs à Agrippa d'Aubigné,* Geneva: Droz, 1969. Doctoral thesis, Univ. of Paris, 1969.
.1 Burgess, R. M., *Ren. Q.,* XXIV (1971), 255–6.
.2 McFarlane, I. D., *FS,* XXV (1971), 321–2.
.3 Mortureaux, B., *Revue des études latines* (1969), 744–5.
.4 Pineaux, J., *RSH* (1971), 314–5.
.5 Thiry, C. J., *RLV,* III (1971), 353–5.

.6 Wilson, D. B., *Erasmus*, XXIII (1971), 92–5.
.7 ..., *YWMLS*, XXXI (1969), 80.

Bd118 ..., *Poésie et mythologie au XVI^esiècle. Quelques mythes de l'inspiration chez les poètes de la Renaissance*, Paris: Nizet, 1969.
.1 Wilson, D. B., *YWMLS*, XXXI (1969), 80.

Bd119 ..., *Orphée et ses disciples dans la poésie française et néo-latine du XVIe siècle*, Geneva: Droz, 1970.
.1 Dottin, G., *RHLF*, LXXI (1971), 494.
.2 Jeanneret, M., *FS*, XXV (1971), 322–3.
.3 Pineaux, J., *RSH*, XXXVI (1971), 315–7.
.4 Richter, M., *St. fr.*, XLII (1970), 528–9.
.5 Scaglione, A., *Rom. Phil.*, XXV (1971–2), 143–4.
.6 Sharratt, P., *YWMLS*, XXXII (1970), 73–4.
.7 Thiry Stassin, M., *RLV*, V (1971), 632–3.
.8 Wagner, F., *Erasmus*, XXIII (1971), 475–6.

Bd120 Jugé, Clément, *Jacques Peletier du Mans (1517–1582). Essai sur sa vie, son œuvre, son influence*, Le Mans: Bienaimé Leguicheux; Paris: Lemerre, 1907. Doctoral thesis, Univ. of Caen, 1906–7.
.1 Plattard, J., *RHLF*, XVIII (1911), 451–2.

Bd121 ..., *Nicolas Denisot du Mans (1515–1559). Essai sur sa vie et ses œuvres*, Le Mans: Bienaimé Leguicheux; Paris: Lemerre, 1907. Thèse complémentaire, Univ. of Caen, 1906–7.
.1 Plattard, J., *RHLF*, XVIII (1911), 451–2.

Bd122 Jung, Marc-René, *Hercule dans la littérature française du XVIe siècle, de l'Hercule courtois à l'Hercule baroque*, Geneva: Droz, 1966. Doctoral thesis, Univ. of Paris, 1964.
.1 Bailbé, J., *RHLF*, LXVIII (1968), 294–5.
.2 McFarlane, I. D., *YWMLS*, XXVIII (1966), 58.
.3 Richter, M., *BHR*, XXVIII (1966), 509–11.
.4 Seznec, J., *FS*, XXIII (1969), 399–400.
.5 Simone, F., *St. fr.*, XXIX (1966), 342.

Bd123 Kastner, Léon E., *A History of French Versification*, Oxford: Clarendon Press, 1903.

Bd124 Katz, Richard A., *Ronsard's French Critics, 1585–1828*, Geneva: Droz, 1966.
.1 McFarlane, I. D., *YWMLS*, XXVIII (1966), 68–9.
.2 Mermier, G., *BHR*, XXX (1968), 381–2.

Bd125 Keating, L. Clark, *Studies on the literary salon in France, 1550–1615*, Cambridge, Mass.: Harvard UP, 1941.

Bd126   Kinch, Charles, *La Poésie satirique de Clément Marot,*
         Paris: Boivin, 1940. Doctoral thesis, Univ. of Paris, 1947.

Bd127   Lachèvre, Frédéric, *Bibliographie des recueils collectifs de*
         poésie du XVIᵉ siècle, Paris: Champion, 1922.
         .1 Chamard, H., *RHLF,* XXX (1923), 550–1.

Bd128   Laumonier, Paul, *Ronsard, poète lyrique; étude historique*
         et littéraire, Paris: Hachette, 1909. Doctoral thesis, Univ.
         of Paris, 1909–10.
         .1 Chamard, H., *RHLF,* XVII (1910), 634–42.
         .2 Cherel, A., *RHLF,* XXXII (1925), 290.
         .3 Tanquerey, F. J., *YWMLS,* I (1931), 47.
         .4 Tilley, A., *MLR,* VI (1911), 268–71.

Bd129   Lawton, H. W., *Terence en France au XVIᵉ siècle.* I:
         Editions et traductions, II: Imitation et influence, Paris:
         Jouve, 1926 (Vol. I); Geneva, 1972 (Vol. II). Doctoral
         thesis, Univ. of Paris, 1926.

Bd130   ..., *Handbook of French Renaissance Dramatic Theory,*
         Manchester UP, 1949.
         .1 Carrington Lancaster, H., *MLN,* LXVI (1951), 205–6.
         .2 Mayer, C. A., *BHR,* XII (1950), 423–4.
         .3 Orr, J., *MLR,* XLVI (1951), 104–5.

Bd131   Lebègue, Raymond, *Ronsard, l'homme et l'œuvre,* Paris:
         Hatier, 1950.
         .1 Becker, G., *Information littéraire,* 3ᵉ année, 3 (1951),
            105.
         .2 Beves, D. H., *MLR,* XLVI (1951), 508–9.

         Leboucher, Louis: see Mounin, Georges.

Bd132   Lee, Sidney, *Elizabethan Sonnets newly arranged and*
         indexed, Westminster, 1904.*
         .1 Thomas, L., *RR,* VI, 5ᵉ année (1905), 61–3.

Bd133   ..., *The French Renaissance in England: An Account of*
         the Literary Relations of England and France in the
         Sixteenth Century, New York, Oxford: Clarendon Press,
         1910.
         .1 Kastner, L. E., *MLR,* VI (1911), 246–53.
         .2 Upham, A. H., *MLN,* XXVI (1911), 177–82.

Bd134   Lefranc, Abel, *Les Lettres et les idées depuis la Renaissance,*
         Paris: Champion, 1914.*

Bd135   Le Hir, Yves, *Esthétique et structure du vers français*
         d'après les théoriciens, du XVIᵉ siècle à nos jours, Paris:
         Presses Universitaires de France, 1956.
         .1 Jourda, P., *RHLF,* LIX (1959), 253–4.

Bd136 . . . , *Rhétorique et stylistique de la Pléiade au Parnasse,* Paris: Presses Universitaires de France, 1960.
.1 McFarlane, I. D., *YWMLS,* XXII (1960), 68.

Bd137 Lejard, Félix-Joseph, *Prosodie française, contenant les règles de la prononciation et de la versification,* Paris: Poussielgue frères, 1888.

Bd138 Lenient, Charles, *La Satire en France ou la littérature militante au XVIe siècle,* Paris: Hachette, 1866.

Bd139 Levengood, Sidney L., *The Use of Color in the Verse of the Pléiade,* Paris: Presses Universitaires de France, 1929. Princeton Dissertation.*

Bd140 Lever, J. W., *The Elizabethan Love Sonnet,* London: Methuen, 1956.
.1 Leech, C., *Durham University Journal,* XVIII (1956–7), 38–40.
.2 Leishman, J. B., *MLR,* LII (1957), 251–5.

Bd141 Levin, Harry, *The Myth of the Golden Age in the Renaissance,* Bloomington: Indiana UP; London: Faber, 1970.
.1 Hill, R. F., *MLR,* LXVII (1972), 159–60.
.2 Hughes, M., *RLC,* XLV (1971), 412–4.
.3 Merivale, P., *Comp. Lit.,* XXIV (1972), 88–90.
.4 Tigerstedt, E. N., *Comp. Lit. Studies,* IX (1972), 102–3.

Bd142 Littleboy, Anna L., *The Relations between French and English Literature in the 16th and 17th centuries,* Lewis, 1895* (London, University College, The Quain Essay, 1895).

Bd143 *Lumières de la Pléiade,* neuvième stage international d'études humanistes, Tours, 1965, Paris: Vrin, 1966. (Introduction by Pierre Mesnard). See Bb245; Be6, 37, 110, 137, 156, 163, 212, 266, 275.
.1 Castor, G. D., *MLR,* LXIV (1969), 165.
.2 Richter, M., *St. fr.,* XXXIII (1967), 528–9.

Bd144 Maddison, Carol H., *Apollo and the Nine. A History of the Ode,* Baltimore: Johns Hopkins Press; London: Routledge and Kegan Paul, 1960. See Bc55.
.1 McFarlane, I. D., *YWMLS,* XXII (1960), 68.
.2 Mombello, G., *St. fr.,* XXIII (1964), 327–8.
.3 Staton, W. F., *Ren. News* (spr. 1962).*

Bd145 Martinon, Philippe, *Les Strophes. Etude historique et critique sur les formes de la poésie lyrique en France depuis la Renaissance, avec une bibliographie chronologique et un répertoire général,* Paris: Champion, 1912.

.1 Madeleine, J., *RHLF,* XXIII (1916), 291–9.

Bd146 Marty-Laveaux, Charles, *La Langue de la Pléiade,* Paris:
A. Lemerre, 1896–8. Published separately, and also as
Appendix to *La Pléiade françoise,* Paris: A. Lemerre, 1866–
98 (20 Vols.). See also Be166.
.1 Larroque, T. de, *Revue critique d'Histoire et de
Littérature* (7.12.1896)*.
.2 Paris, G., *Journal des Savants* (May 1898)*.

Bd147 Maugain, Gabriel, *Ronsard en Italie,* Paris: Les Belles
Lettres, 1926.
.1 Cohen, G., *RLC,* IX (1929), 610–2.

Bd148 Mehnert, Kurt-Henning, *Sal Romanus und Esprit Français:
Studien zur Martialreception im Frankreich des 16. und 17.
Jahrhunderts,* Bonn: Romanisches Seminar der Universität
Bonn, 1970. Doctoral thesis, Univ. of Bonn, 1969.
.1 Hausmann, F. R., *Archiv,* CXXIV (1972), 455–7.

Bd149 Ménage, Gilles, *Anti-Baillet, ou critique du livre de Mr
Baillet, intitulé Jugemens des Savans,* The Hague, 1688.*
See Bb11.

Bd150 Ménager, Daniel, *Introduction à la vie littéraire au XVIe
siècle,* Paris: Bordas/Mouton, 1968.

Bd151 Merrill, Robert V., and R. J. Clements, *Platonism in
French Renaissance Poetry,* New York UP, 1957.
.1 England, S. L., *YWMLS,* XIX (1957), 71–2.
.2 Lebègue, R., *Ren. News,* XI (1958), 146–8.
.3 Silver, I., *MLN,* LXXIII (1958), 175–7.
.4 Sozzi, L., *St. fr.,* IX (1959), 472–3.

Mesnard, Pierre: see Bd143.

Bd152 Meylan, Henri, *Epîtres du Coq à l'Ane. Contribution à
l'histoire de la satire au XVIe siècle,* Geneva: Droz, 1956.
.1 England, S. L., *YWMLS,* XVIII (1956), 62.
.2 Grève, M. de, *RBPH,* I (1957) *.
.3 Sozzi, L., *St. fr.,* VI (1958), 481.

Bd153 Mönch, Walter, *Frankreichs Dichtung von der Renaissance
zur Gegenwart im Spiegel geistesgeschichtlicher Probleme,*
Berlin: E. Ebering, 1933.*

Bd154 . . . , *Die italienische Platonrenaissance und ihre Bedeutung
für Frankreichs Literatur- und Geistesgeschichte 1450–
1550,* Berlin: E. Ebering, 1936.*

Bd155 . . . , *Frankreichs Literatur im XVI Jahrhundert. Eine
nationalpolitische Geistesgeschichte der französischen
Renaissance,* Berlin: W. de Gruyter & Co., 1938.*

Bd156   ..., *Das Sonett, Gestalt und Geschichte,* Heidelberg:
F. H. Kerle, 1955.
.1 Bémol, M., *RHLF,* LVII (1957), 293–4.
.1a Giudicci, E., *St. fr.,* V (1958), 297. (CR of Bémol).
.2 Morón. G., *Revista Nacional de Cultura,* Caracas (Mar.–
Apr. 1955).
.3 Voisine, J., *RLC,* XXXIV (1960), 324–30.

Bd157   Molinier, H.-J., *Mellin de Saint-Gelays (1490? –1558).
Etude sur sa vie et ses œuvres,* Paris, Rodez, 1910.
Doctoral thesis, Univ. of Toulouse, 1909–10.

Bd158   Morçay, Raoul, and Armand Müller, *La Renaissance*
[*Histoire de la littérature française,* published under the
direction of J. Calvet], Paris: del Duca, 1960. See Bb167.

Bd159   Mounin, Georges (pseud. of Louis Leboucher), *Les Belles
Infidèles,* Paris: Cahiers du Sud, 1955. [The art of
translation].

Bd160   Müller, Armand, *La Poésie religieuse catholique de
Marot à Malherbe,* Paris: Imprimerie de R. Foulon, 1950.
See Bb171.

Bd161   Murăraşu, D., *La Poésie néo-latine et la Renaissance des
lettres antiques en France 1500–1549,* Paris: J. Gamber,
1926.
.1 Jourda, P., *RHLF,* XXXVI (1929), 278–80.

Bd162   *Musique et poésie au XVIe siècle* (Colloques internationaux
du C.R.N.S. Sciences humaines V, 30 juin – 4 juillet
1953), ed. Jean Jacquot, Paris: Edns du C.N.R.S., 1954.
.1 Rousset, J., *RLC,* XXXIV (1960), 315–6.

Bd163   Naïs, Hélène, *Les Animaux dans la littérature française de
la Renaissance. Science, symbolique, poésie,* Paris: Didier,
1961.
.1 Ehrard, J., *Annales,* XVIII (1963), 196–8.*
.2 Guiette, R., *RBPH,* XLII (1964), 143–5.
.3 Lebègue, R., *RHLF,* LXIII (1963), 123–5.
.4 McFarlane, I. D., *FS,* XVIII (1964), 151–4.
.5 ..., *YWMLS,* XXIII (1961), 59.
.6 Mermier, G., *BHR,* XXV (1963), 282–4.
.7 Schön, P. M., *Romanische Forschungen,* LXXV (1963),
459–61.
.8 Sozzi, L., *St. fr.,* XXV (1965), 134.
.9 Terreaux, L., *FM,* XXXI (1963), 228–31.

Bd164   Naïs, Hélène, Sem Dresden and Michael Screech, *Invention
et imitation. Etudes sur la littérature du seizième siècle*
(sous la direction de J. A. G. Tans), The Hague; Brussels:

Van Goor Zonen, 1968.
.1 Coleman, D., *FS*, XXIV (1970), 283–4.
.2 Jeanneret, M., *BHR*, XXXI (1969), 398.
.3 Pineaux, J., *RHLF,* LXIX (1969), 1023–4.
.4 Richter, M., *St. fr.*, XL (1970), 134–5.

Bd165   Neri, Ferdinando, *Il Chiabrera e la Pléiade francese,* Turin: fratelli Bocca, 1920.
.1 Kastner, L. E., *MLR*, XVI (1921), 372.
.2 Plattard, J., *RSS*, VIII (1921), 152–3.
.3 Potez, H., *RHLF*, XXIX (1922), 366–8.

Bd166   Nerval, Gérard de, *Les Poètes du XVIe siècle* (texte de 1831, *Mercure de France*, éd. M. Françon), Cambridge, Mass.: Schoenhof's Foreign Books, 1959.

Bd167   Niceron, Jean Pierre, *Mémoires pour servir à l'histoire des hommes illustres dans la république des lettres, avec un catalogue raisonné de leurs ouvrages,* Paris, 1727–45.* (43 tomes = 44 vols. Tome X has 2 parts. For Du B. see vols. XVI and XX).

Bd168   Nolhac, Pierre de, *Ronsard et l'humanisme,* Paris: Champion, 1921.
.1 Hauvette, H., *RLC*, II (1922), 660–3.
.2 Johnson, F. C., *MLR*, XX (1925), 95–6.
.3 Plattard, J., *RSS*, IX (1922), 83–6.
.4 Schoell, F. L., *MP*, XIX (1921–2), 428–9.

Bd169   Noot, Jan van der, *Le Théâtre auquel sont exposés et monstrés les inconveniens & miseres qui suivent les mondains & vicieux, . . . ,* London: J. Day, 1568.*

Bd170   *. . . , A Theatre, wherein be represented as wel the miseries & calamities that follow the voluptuous Worldlings, as also the greate joyes and plesures which the faithful do enjoy, . . . ,* Devised by S. J. van-der-Noot. (Translated out of French by T. Roest), London: H. Bynnemann, 1569.* Facsimile copy, New York, 1936.*

Bd171   O'Connor, Dorothy, *Louise Labé, sa vie et son œuvre,* Abbeville, Paris: Les presses françaises, 1926. Doctoral thesis, Univ. of Paris, 1926.

Bd172   Opitz von Boberfeld, Martin, *M. Opitii Buch von der Deutschen Poeterey,* Brieg, 1624.*

Bd173   Osborne, Nancy F., *The Doctor in the French Literature of the Sixteenth Century,* New York: King's Crown Press; Oxford UP, 1946.
.1 Lawton, H. W., *MLR*, XLII (1947), 278.

Paris, L.: see Bd103.

Bd174 Pasquier, Etienne, *Les Œuvres d'Estienne Pasquier contenant ses Recherches de la France, . . . ,* Amsterdam: Trévoux, 1723.

Bd175 *. . . , Choix de lettres sur la littérature, la langue et la traduction* (ed. D. Thickett), Geneva: Droz, 1956.
.1 Armstrong, E., *FS,* XI (1957), 347–9.
.2 Lawton, H. W., *MLR,* LII (1957), 437–8.
.3 Meylan, H., *BHR,* XIX (1957), 154.

Bd176 Patterson, Warner F., *Three Centuries of French Poetic Theory,* Michigan UP, 1935.
.1 Lawton, H. W., *YWMLS,* VII (1937), 46.
.2 Legge, J. G., *MLR,* XXXI (1936), 590–2.
.3 Weinberg, B., *MP,* XXXIV (1936–7), 319–22.

Bd177 Peyre, Roger, *Une Princesse de la Renaissance. Marguerite de France, duchesse de Berry, duchesse de Savoie,* Paris: Paut et Guillen, 1902.*

Bd178 Picot, Emile, *Les Français italianisants au XVIe siècle,* Paris: Champion, 1906–7.

Bd179 Piéri, Marius, *Le Pétrarquisme au XVIe siècle. Pétrarque et Ronsard, ou de l'influence de Pétrarque sur la Pléiade française,* Marseille: Lafitte, 1896; Geneva: Droz, 1970. Doctoral thesis, Univ. of Paris, 1895–6.

Bd180 Pineaux, Jacques, *La Poésie des protestants de langue française (1559–1598),* Paris: Klincksieck, 1972.

Bd181 Pinvert, Lucien, *Jacques Grévin (1538–1570): sa vie, ses écrits, ses amis. Etude biographique et littéraire,* Paris: Fontemoing, 1898. Doctoral thesis, Univ. of Nancy, 1898–9.

Bd182 Rathery, E. J. B., *L'Influence de l'Italie sur les lettres françaises depuis le XIIIe siècle jusqu'au règne de Louis XIV,* Paris: Didot, 1853.

Bd183 Raymond, Marcel, *L'Influence de Ronsard sur la poésie française (1550–1585),* Paris: Champion, 1927; Geneva: Droz, 1965. Doctoral thesis, Univ. of Paris, 1927.
.1 Laumonier, P., *RHLF,* XXXVII (1930), 97–104.
.2 Lebègue, R., *Revue critique,* XCV (1928), 221–4.
.3 Lefranc, A., *RSS,* XIV (1927), 414–7.
.4 McFarlane, I. D., *YWMLS,* XXVII (1965), 63.
.5 Richter, M., *St. fr.,* XXVIII (1966), 132.
.6 Tanquerey, F. J., *YWMLS,* I (1931), 48.
.7 Weber, H., *RHLF,* LXVII (1967), 806.

Bd184 Rehm, W., *Europäische Romdichtung*, Munich: Max Huebler, 1939. See Bb204.

Bd185 Richter, Mario, *Giovanni Della Casa in Francia nel secolo XVI*, Rome, 1966.
.1 Sozzi, L., *St. fr.*, XXXIII (1967), 526–7.

Bd186 ..., *La poesia lirica in Francia nel secolo XVI*, Milan-Varese: Istituto editoriale cisalpino, 1971.
.1 Lauvergnat, C., *BHR*, XXXV (1973), 149–51.

Bd187 Rickard, Peter, *La Langue française au seizième siècle. Etude suivie de textes*, Cambridge UP, 1968.
.1 Baumgartner, E., *Rom. Phil.*, XXVI (1972–3), 146–8.
.2 Borella, L., *St. fr.*, XLII (1970), 527–8.
.3 Bowen, B. C., *MLR*, LXIV (1969), 421–2.
.4 Catach, N., *BHR*, XXXI (1969), 248–9.
.5 Wilson, D. B., *YWMLS*, XXX (1968), 41.

Bd188 Rimski-Korsakov, W., *Histoire de la littérature française*, Académie des Sciences de l'U.R.S.S., 1946.*

Bd189 Rossettini-Trtnik, Olga, *Les Influences anciennes et italiennes sur la satire en France au XVIe siècle*, Florence, 1958. Doctoral thesis, Univ. of Paris, 1953.
.1 Giudici, E., *St. fr.*, XI (1960), 296–7.
.2 Lebègue, R., *RLC*, XXXV (1961), 299–302.
.3 Weber, H., *RHLF*, LX (1960), 231–2.

Bd190 Roy, Loys le, *Le Sympose de Platon, ... traduit ... avec trois livres de commentaires, ... par Loys Le Roy, dit Regius, ...*, Paris: J. Longis et R. Le Mangnyer, 1558.

Bd191 Rucktäschel, Theodor, *Einige Arts Poëtiques aus der Zeit Ronsard's und Malherbe's. Ein Beitrag zur Geschichte der französischen Poetik des 16. und 17. Jahrhunderts*, Leipzig: Gustav Frock, 1889. Doctoral thesis, Univ. of Leipzig, 1889.

Bd192 Sainte-Beuve, Charles-Augustin, *Tableau historique et critique de la poésie française et du théâtre français au XVIe siècle*, Paris: Charpentier, 1828.

Bd193 ..., *Correspondance*, Paris: Calmann Lévy, 1878. (Tome II, p.247, Lettre à Révillout à propos de son mémoire "Des derniers mois de Du B."). See Bb207.

Bd194 Saulnier, Verdun L., *La Littérature française de la Renaissance (1500–1610)*, Paris: Presses Universitaires de France, 1942.
.1 Sozzi, L., *St. fr.*, XIX (1963), 136.

Bd195   ..., *Maurice Scève (ca. 1500–1560),* Paris: Klincksieck, 1948.

Bd196   ..., *Paris devant la Renaissance des lettres,* Paris: Société d'édition d'enseignement supérieur, 1951.

Bd197   Schaar, Claes, *On the motiv of death in 16th-century sonnet poetry,* Lund: Gleerup, 1960.

Bd198   Schroeder, V., *Quid de moribus studiis et latine scribendi genere Michaelis Hospitalis ex ejusdem carminibus concludi possit,* Paris: Hachette, 1899.

Bd199   Schutz, Alexander H., *Vernacular Books in Parisian Private Libraries of the Sixteenth Century according to the Notarial Inventories,* Univ. of N. Carolina Studies in Romance Languages and Literatures, 25, Chapel Hill, 1955.
.1 England, S. L., *YWMLS,* XVIII (1956), 56.
.2 Lebègue, R., *RHLF,* LVIII (1958), 534–5.

Bd200   Schweinitz, Margaret de, *Les Epitaphes de Ronsard (Etude historique et littéraire),* Paris: Presses Universitaires de France, 1925. Doctoral thesis, Univ. of Paris, 1925.
.1 Laumonier, P., *MLN,* LXI (1926), 60–3.
.2 Tanquerey, F. J., *YWMLS,* I (1931), 47.

Bd201   Scollen, C. M., *The Birth of the Elegy in France,* Geneva: Droz, 1967. M. Phil. thesis, Bedford College, Univ. of London, 1967.
.1 Camproux, C., *RLR,* LXXVIII (1968), 191–2.
.2 Desonay, F., *RBPH,* XLVII (1969), 541–3.
.3 Graham, V. E., *Rom. Rev.,* LX (1969), 196–7.
.4 Hallowell, R. E., *Ren. Q.,* XXII (1969), 168–70.
.5 McFarlane, I. D., *FS,* XXIII (1969), 280–1.
.6 Mermier, G., *BHR,* XXXI (1969), 429–30.
.7 Ortali, R., *FR,* XLII (1968–9), 317–8.
.8 Richter, M., *St. fr.,* XXXV (1968), 340.
.9 Schulz-Buschhaus, V., *Rom. Jahrb.,* XX (1969), 198–201.
.10 Stone, D., *MLQ,* XXX (1969), 132–3.
.11 Wilson, D. B., *YWMLS,* XXIX (1967), 46.

Screech, Michael A: see Bd164.

Bd202   Silver, Isidore, *Pindaric Odes of Ronsard,* Paris: P. André, 1937. Doctoral thesis, Univ. of Columbia, 1938.
.1 Tilley, A., *MLR,* XXXV (1940), 133.

Bd203   ..., *Ronsard and the Hellenic Renaissance in France. I Ronsard and the Greek Epic,* St Louis: Washington UP,

1961.
.1 Aulotte, R., *RHLF,* LXIII (1963), 467–8.
.2 Bensimon, M., *St. fr.,* XXVIII (1966), 91–5.
.3 Dassonville, M., *BHR,* XXV (1963), 441–8.
.4 Lytton Sells, A., *MLN,* LXXIX (1964), 320–2.
.5 McFarlane, I. D., *YWMLS,* XXIII (1961), 59.
.6 . . . , *YWMLS,* XXIV (1962), 81.

Bd204 . . . , *The Intellectual Evolution of Ronsard. I: The Formative Influences,* St. Louis: Washington UP, 1969.
.1 Castor, G. D., *FS,* XXVI (1972), 71–3.
.2 Katz, R. A., *Rom. Rev.,* LXIII (1972), 45–7.
.3 Quainton, M., *MLR,* LXVII (1972), 631–4.
.4 Stone, D., *MLN,* LXXXV (1970), 608–9.
.5 Terreaux, L., *RHLF,* LXXII (1972), 301–3.

Bd205 Simone, Franco, *Il Rinascimento francese: studi e richerche,* Turin, 1961.
.1 Klein, R., *BHR,* XXIII (1961), 646–9.
.2 McFarlane, I. D., *YWMLS,* XXIII (1961), 56.
.3 Mombello, G., *RHLF,* LXII (1962), 597–9.
.4 Moreau, P., *RLC,* XXXV (1961), 649–52.

Bd206 . . . , *Umanesimo, Rinascimento, Barocco in Francia,* Milan, 1968.
.1 Bailbé, J., *RHLF,* LXX (1970), 121–2.
.2 Cave, T., *MLR,* LXVI (1971), 183–4.
.3 McFarlane, I. D., *FS,* XXV (1971), 323–5.
.4 Mombello, G., *RLC,* XLV (1971), 262–7.

Bd207 . . . , *The French Renaissance. Medieval Tradition and Italian Influence in Shaping the Renaissance in France* (translated by H. G. Hall), London, 1969.
.1 Coleman, D., *MLR,* LXVI (1971), 404–6.
.2 McFarlane, I. D., *FS,* XXV (1971), 323–5.

Bd208 Smith, Pauline M., *The Anti-Courtier Trend in Sixteenth-Century French Literature,* Geneva: Droz, 1966. Doctoral thesis, Bedford College, Univ. of London, 1964.
.1 McFarlane, I. D., *YWMLS,* XXVIII (1966), 58.

Bd209 Sozzi, Lionello, *La Polémique anti-italienne en France au XVIe siècle,* Turin: Accademia delle Scienze, 1972.
.1 Yardeni, M., *BHR,* XXXV (1973), 178–9.

Bd210 Spingarn, Joel E., *A History of literary criticism in the Renaissance, with special reference to the influence of Italy in the formation and development of modern classicism,* New York: Macmillan, 1899.*
.1 Bouvy, E., *Bull. it.,* I, (1901), 159–62.

Bd211   Stapfer, Paul, *Victor Hugo et la grande poésie satirique en France,* Paris: P. Ollendorf, 1901.*

Bd212   Stirner, Berta, *Ariost und die französische Poesie der Renaissance,* Münster, 1931.
.1 Tanquerey, F. J., *YWMLS,* III (1933), 47.

Bd213   Stone, Donald, *Ronsard's Sonnet Cycles: A Study in Tone and Vision,* New Haven and London: Yale UP, 1966.
.1 Burgess, R. M., *MP,* LXV (1967–8), 155–6.
.2 Gadoffre, G., *MLR,* LXIII (1968), 247–9.
.3 Lawton, H. W., *FS,* XXI (1967), 339–40.
.4 McFarlane, I. D., *YWMLS,* XXVIII (1966), 67.
.5 Weber, H., *RHLF,* LXVIII (1968), 97–8.

Bd214   . . . , *France in the Sixteenth Century - A Medieval Society Transformed,* Prentice-Hall, New Jersey: Spectrum Paperback, 1969.

Bd215   Strowski, Fortunat J., *La Pléiade: la doctrine et l'œuvre poétique,* Paris: Centre de documentation universitaire, 1933.

Bd216   Tardieu, Jean, and Urbano Cioccetti, *Les Français à Rome, résidents et voyageurs dans la Ville Éternelle de la Renaissance au début du Romantisme,* Paris, 1961.*
.1 Gautier, J. M., *BHR,* XXIV (1962), 266–8.

Bd217   Taylor, Henry O., *Thought and Expression in the Sixteenth Century,* New York: Macmillan, 1920.

Bd218   Terreaux, Louis, *Ronsard, correcteur de ses œuvres: Les variantes des odes et des deux premiers livres des "Amours",* Geneva: Droz, 1968.

Thickett, D.: see Bd175.

Bd219   Thieme, Hugo P., *Essai sur l'histoire du vers français,* Paris: Champion, 1916.*

Bd220   Thornton, Frances C., *The French Element in Spenser's Poetical Works,* Toulouse: Lion & fils, 1938.* Doctoral thesis, Univ. of Toulouse, 1938.

Bd221   Tieghem, Philippe van, *Petite histoire des grandes doctrines littéraires en France. De la Pléiade au surréalisme,* Paris: Presses Universitares de France, 1946.
.1 Bray, R., *RHLF,* XLVIII (1948), 276–7.

Bd222   Tilley, Arthur A., *Studies in the French Renaissance,* Cambridge UP, 1922.

Bd223   Trousson, Raymond, *Le Thème de Prométhée dans la littérature européenne*, Geneva: Droz, 1962.
.1 McFarlane, I. D., *YWMLS*, XXVI (1964), 62.
.2 Pollard, P., *MLR*, LXIII (1968), 661–2.

Bd224   Turner, Robert E., *Didon dans la tragédie de la Renaissance italienne et française*, Paris: Fouillot, 1926. Doctoral thesis, Univ. of Paris, 1926.

Bd225   Upham, Alfred H., *The French Influence in English Literature from the Accession of Elizabeth to the Restoration*, New York: Macmillan, 1899, 1911.*

Bd226   Vaganay, Hugues, *Le Sonnet en Italie et en France au XVIe siècle. Essai de bibliographie comparée*, Lyon: Bibliothèque des Facultés catholiques de Lyon, 1902–3.
.1 Vianey, J., *RHLF*, IX (1902), 696.

Bd227   . . . , Lodge et Desportes [Stanzas from Desportes *Premières œuvres*, 1576, with the translation by T. Lodge. Edited by H.V.], 1922.* (No place of publication given).

Bd228   Vernier, P., *Le Vers français: I. La formation du poème, II. Les Mètres, III. Adaptations germaniques*, Paris, 1931–2.*

Bd229   Vianey, Joseph, *Mathurin Régnier*, Paris: Hachette, 1896.

Bd230   . . . , *Le Pétrarquisme en France au XVIe siècle*, Montpellier: Coulet, 1909.
.1 Laumonier, P., *RHLF*, XVII (1910), 859–63.

Bd231   . . . , *Les Odes de Ronsard*, Paris: SFELT, 1932.
.1 Tanquerey, F. J., *YWMLS*, IV (1934), 47.

Bd232   Weber, Henri, *La Création poétique au XVIe siècle en France de Maurice Scève à Agrippa d'Aubigné*, Paris: Nizet, 1955.
.1 England, S. L., *YWMLS*, XVIII (1956), 58.
.2 Françon, M., *MLN*, LXXIII (1958), 227–9.
.3 Giudici, E., *St. fr.*, II (1957), 272–6.
.4 Lawton, H. W., *FS*, XI (1957), 344–6.
.5 Portier, L., *Revue des études italiennes*, IV (1957), 260–3.
.6 Silver, I., *Rom. Rev.*, XLVIII (1957), 122–6.

Bd233   Weinberg, Bernard, *Critical Prefaces of the French Renaissance*, Evanston, Illinois: Northwestern UP, 1950.
.1 Carrington Lancaster, H., *MLN*, LXVI (1951), 205–6.
.2 Lebègue, R., *RHLF*, LIII (1953), 371–2.
.3 Orr, J., *MLR*, XLVI (1951), 104–5.

.4 Peyre, H., *MP*, XLVIII (1950–1), 273.
.5 Saulnier, V. L., *BHR*, XII (1950), 387–90.

Bd234 Weise, Georg, *L'ideale eroico del Rinascimento. Diffusione europea e tramonto*, Naples: Edizioni Scientifiche Italiane, 1965.
.1 Pellegrini, G., *Rivista di letteratura moderne e comparate*, XX (1967), 62–6.

Bd235 Wiley, William L., *The Gentlemen of Renaissance France*, Cambridge, Mass.: Harvard UP, 1954.
.1 Clements, R. J., *MLN*, LXX (1955), 308–12.

Bd236 Willey, Basil, *Tendencies in Renaissance Literary Theories*, Cambridge: Bowes and Bowes, 1922.

Bd237 Wilson, Dudley B., *Ronsard, Poet of Nature*, Manchester UP, 1961.
.1 Desonay, F., *RHLF*, LXII (1962), 600–1.
.2 McFarlane, I. D., *YWMLS*, XXIII (1961), 60.
.3 Silver, I., *BHR*, XXIV (1962), 528–30.
.4 Sozzi, L., *St. fr.*, XV (1961), 535–6.
.5 Walker, D. P., *MLR*, LVII (1962), 440–1.

Bd238 . . . , *Descriptive Poetry in France from Blason to Baroque*, Manchester UP, 1967.
.1 Bailbé, J., *RHLF*, LXIX (1969), 125–6.
.2 Chesney, K., *FS*, XXII (1968), 243.
.3 Joukovsky, F., *BHR*, XXIX (1967), 744–5.
.4 Richter, M., *St. fr.*, XXXVI (1968), 529–30.
.5 Stone, D., *MLR*, LXIII (1968), 964–5.
.6 Wilson, D. B., *YWMLS*, XXIX (1967), 46–7.

Bd239 Wind, Bartina H., *Les Mots italiens introduits en français au XVIe siècle*, Deventer: E. Kluwer, 1928.

Bd240 Witton, Marianne, *Das Nationalisierungs Programm der französischen Renaissance auf dem Gebiet der Sprache, Dichkunst, Religion und Sitte*, Coburg, 1940. Doctoral thesis, Univ. of Breslau, 1940.

Bd241 Wolf, Lothar (ed.), *Texte und Dokumente zur französischen Sprachgeschichte. 16. Jahrhundert*, Tübingen: Max Niemeyer, 1969.

Bd242 Wyndham, George, *Ronsard & la Pléiade, with selections from their poetry and some translations in the original metres*, London: Macmillan, 1906. Also in *Essays in Romantic Literature*, London: Macmillan, 1919.
.1 Tilley, A., *MLR*, II (1906–7), 260.

Bd243   Wyndham Lewis, D. B., *Ronsard*, London: Sheed & Ward, 1944.

.1 Bisson, L. A., *MLR*, XL (1945), 60–3.

ARTICLES AND CHAPTERS OF BOOKS
IN WHICH SIGNIFICANT REFERENCE IS MADE TO DU BELLAY

* * *

Be1   Anon., 'The Pléiade and the Elizabethan', *Edinburgh Review,* CCV (1907), 353–79.*

Be2   Anon., [S. A. -B., Munich], 'Ronsard and the Poets of the Pléiade', *The Academy,* 2016 (24.12.10), 611–2; 2017 (31.12.10), 639–40.

Be3   Arnold, Ivor D. O., 'Sainte-Beuve's *Tableau de la poésie française au XVIᵉ siècle* and Cary's *Early French Poets*', in *Studies . . . presented to Graeme Ritchie,* Cambridge UP, 1949, pp. 1–8.

Be4   Aulotte, Robert, 'Sur quelques traductions d'une ode de Sappho au XVIᵉ siècle', *BGB* (Dec. 1958), 107–22. Résumé, under title 'La fortune d'une ode de Sappho au XVIᵉ siècle' in *Ass. G. Budé,* Congrès de Lyon (8–13 Sept. 1958), Paris: Les Belles Lettres, 1960, pp. 444–6.
    .1 Sozzi, L., *St. fr.,* VIII (1959), 301.

Be5   . . . , 'Une défense manuscrite de la langue française au XVIᵉ siècle', *BHR,* XXVII (1965), 513–22.
    .1 McFarlane, I. D., *YWMLS,* XXVII (1965), 61.

Be6   . . . , 'Amyot et la Pléiade ', in Bd143, pp. 63–73.

Be7   Bailbé, Jacques, 'Le Thème de la vieille femme dans la poésie satirique du seizième et du début du dix-septième siècle', *BHR,* XXVI (1964), 98–119.

Be8   . . . , 'Le Courtisan sous Henri III et Henri IV', *Ass. G. Budé,* Congrès de Paris, Paris: Les Belles Lettres, 1969, pp. 675–7. Résumé of lecture.
    .1 Richter, M., *St. fr.,* XLIII (1971), 130–1.

B39   Baillou, Jean, 'L'influence de la pensée philosophique de la Renaissance italienne sur la pensée française. Etat présent des travaux relatifs au XVIᵉ siècle', *Revue des études italiennes,* I (1936), 116–155.

Be10   Balmas, Enea, 'Il mito della "Pléiade" ', *Saggi e richerche di letteratura francese,* VI (1965), 9–36.
    .1 Richter, M., *St. fr.,* XXIX (1966), 337.

Be11   Baron, Hans, 'The *Querelle* of the Ancients and the Moderns as a problem for Renaissance Scholarship', in *Renaissance Essays*, ed. Paul O. Kristeller and Philip P. Wiener, New York: Harper Torchbooks, 1968, pp. 95–114.

Be12   Batault, Georges, 'Le Problème de la culture et la crise de français', *Mercure de France*, XCII (July 1911), 52–81.

Be13   Beall, Chandler B., 'Some Aspects of Petrarchism', in *Actes du Ve congrès de l'Association internationale de littérature comparée* (Belgrade 1967), Amsterdam: Swets & Zeitlinger, 1969, pp. 73–8.
    .1 Beller, M., *Arcadia*, VI, 3 (1971), 187–92.

Be14   Bellesort, André, 'L'Hôtellerie', *RDM*, LXV (1895), 223–9. [Poem on the meeting of Du B. and Ronsard].

Be15   Benesch, Otto, 'The Ancient and the Gothic Revival in French Art and Literature', in Bd90, pp. 209–28.

Be16   Bensimon, Marc, 'The significance of eye imagery in the Renaissance from Bosch to Montaigne', *Yale French Studies*, XLVII (1972), 266–89.

Be17   Berdan, John M., and Léon E. Kastner, 'Wyatt and the French Sonneteers', *MLR*, IV (1908–9), 240–53.

Be18   Bertoni, Giulio, 'L'ispiratrice della Pléiade', in *Spunti, Scorci e commenti* (Biblioteca dell' "Archivum Romanicum", 10), Geneva: Leo S. Olschki, 1928, pp. 49–54.

Be19   Besch, Emile, 'Un moraliste satirique et rationaliste au XVIe siècle. Jacques Tahureau (1527–1555)', *RSS*, VI (1918), 1–44, 157–200.

Be20   Blechmann, Wilhelm, 'Imitatio Creatrix bei Ronsard, zum Sonett "Quand vous serez bien vieille", *Sonnets pour Hélène*, II, 43', *ZFSL*, LXXIII, (1963), 1–16.
    .1 Drost, W., *St. fr.*, XXV (1965), 140.

Be21   Brachin, Pierre, 'Un disciple de Ronsard: Jan vander Noot "patrice d'Anvers" ', *Archives de lettres modernes*, III, 24 (June–July 1959), 1–35.

Be22   Braye, L., 'Notes sur la Pléiade dans le Barrois, Pantaléon Thévenin, et Clovis Hestaux de Nuisement', *Annales de l'est* (Annuaire fédér. lorr.), I (1928), 61–70.*

Be23   Brunetière, Ferdinand, 'La Pléiade française', *RDM*, CLXII (15.12.1900), 899–919, contd. in *RDM*, n.s. I (1901), 141–66, 660–76.

Be24   . . . , 'L'Œuvre de la Pléiade', *Revue Fribourg*, IV (1905), 81–108.*

Be25   Brunot, Ferdinand, 'Un projet d' "enrichir, magnifier et publier" la langue française en 1509', *RHLF,* I (1894), 27–37.

Be26   Budagow, R. A., 'La Normalisation de la langue littéraire en France au XVIe et XVIIe siècles', *BRP,* I (1961), 143–58.

Be27   Burgess, R. M., 'The Sonnet – a cosmopolitan literary form – in the Renaissance' in *Actes du IVe congrès de l'Association internationale de littérature comparée,* I, 1966, pp. 169–84.*

Be28   Camproux, Charles, 'Bellaud et la Pléiade ', *Annales de l'Institut d'Etudes Occitanes* (1960), 54–7.*
        .1 Mombello, G., *St. fr.,* XX (1963), 338.

Be29   Cannings, Barbara C., 'Les Caractéristiques essentielles de la farce française et leur survivance dans les années 1550–1620', *AUP,* XXXIII (1963), 488. Résumé of Bd24.

Be30   Carrington Lancaster, H., 'Deux sonnets attribués à Ronsard et à Hélène de Surgères', in *Adventures of a Literary Historian,* Baltimore: Johns Hopkins Press, 1942, pp. 166–73.

Be31   Cave, Terence C., 'The Love-Sonnets of Jean de Sponde – a Reconsideration', *FMLS,* III (1967), 49–60.

Be32   Cerreta, F., 'The Italian Origin of the "sonnet régulier" ', *BHR,* XXI (1959), 301–10.

Be33   Chamard, Henri, 'Introduction à l'histoire de la Pléiade. Vue d'ensemble sur la poésie française de 1328–1549' (Leçon d'ouverture, Dec. 1898), *Bulletin de l'Université de Lille* (Jan. 1899).*

Be34   . . . , 'Sonnets chrétiens inédits de Lancelot de Carle Evêque de Riez', in *Mélanges . . . Gustave Lanson,* Paris: Hachette, 1922, pp. 87–97.

Be35   . . . , 'Introduction à une histoire de la Pléiade. Considérations bibliographiques', *RHLF,* XL (1933), 481–96; XLI (1934), 1–14, 321–43.
        .1 Lawton, H. W., *YWMLS,* V (1935), 53.

Be36   Charlier, M. G., 'Jean Le Blond et son apologie de la langue française', *Revue de l'instruction publique en Belgique* (1912?).*
        .1 Plattard, J., *RSS,* I (1913), 447.

Be37   Cioranescu, Alexandre I., 'La Pléiade et le poème épique', in Bd143, pp. 75–86.

Be38   Clédat, Léon, 'Le Musée de sculpture du Cardinal Du B. à Rome (Document tiré des archives d'état à Rome)', *Courrier de l'art*, III (1883), 99–100, 206–7.

Be39   Cledina, Rapha, 'Rabelais et l'aiguille de Virgile à Rome', *RSS*, XVI (1929), 122–32.

Be40   Clement, N. H., 'The First French Sonneteer', *Rom. Rev.*, XIV (1923), 189–98.

Be41   Clements, Robert J., 'Pléiade censure of classic mendacity', *PMLA*, LVI (1941), 633–44.

Be42   . . . , 'Literary Quarrels and Cavils: A Theme of Renaissance Emblem Books', *MLN*, LXX (1955), 549–58.

Be43   . . . , 'Iconography and the nature and inspiration of poetry in Renaissance emblem literature', *PMLA*, LXX (1955), 781–804.

Be44   . . . , and Robert V. Merrill, 'Antipetrarchism in the Pléiade', *MP*, XXXIX (1941–2), 15–21.

Be45   Clerc, Charles, 'La Pléiade à Genève', *Journal des Débats* (4.12.25).*

Be46   Cogan-Bernstein, F.,'La Lutte pour la langue nationale dans l'humanisme français', *Recherches soviétiques* (no. 4 Histoire des idées) (May–June 1956).*

Be47   Coleman, Dorothy, 'Images in Scève's *Délie*', *MLR*, LIX (1964), 375–86.
        .1 Richter, M., *St. fr.*, XXVI (1965), 338.

Be48   Condeescu, N. N., 'Le Paradoxe bernesque dans la littérature française de la Renaissance', *BRP*, II (1963), 27–51.

Be49   Costil, P., 'La Question homérique et l'évolution du goût littéraire en France', *Annales de l'Université de Grenoble*, n.s. XIX (1943), 95–168.*

Be50   Cuervo, R. J., 'Dos poesías de Quevedo á Roma', *Revue Hispanique*, XVIII (1908), 434–8.

Be51   Dargan, E. Preston, 'Trissino, a possible source for the Pléiade', *MP*, XIII (1915–6), 685–8.

Be52   Dassonville, Michel, 'La Collaboration de la Pléiade à la dialectique de Pierre de la Ramée', *BHR*, XXV (1963), 337–48.
        .1 McFarlane, I. D., *YWMLS*, XXV (1963), 44.
        .2 Mombello, G., *St. fr.*, XXV (1964), 139.

Be53 Davis, M. Gerard, 'A Humanist Family in the Sixteenth Century', in *The French Mind. Studies in Honour of Gustave Rudler*, Oxford: Clarendon Press, 1952, pp. 1–16.

Be54 Dawkins, Jasmine, 'The sea in 16th -century French poetry', *Nottingham French Studies*, IX (1970), 3–15.

Be54 Dawson, John C., 'Bernard de Poey. A contemporary of the Pléiade', *Rom. Rev.*, XIV (1923), 119–30.

Be56 Délboulle, A., 'Historique du mot "patrie" ', *RHLF*, VIII (1901), 688–9.

Be57 Delumeau, Jean, 'Contribution à l'histoire des Français à Rome pendant le XVIᵉ siècle', *Mélanges d'archéologie et d'histoire*, XLIV (1952), 249–86.*

Be58 Deschamps, Gaston, 'Ronsard au Collège de Coqueret', *RCC*, X (1902), 584–91.

Be59 . . . , 'Ronsard et ses amis: leurs divertissements et leurs lectures au Collège de Coqueret. L'*Art poétique* de Th. Sibilet', *RCC*, X (1902), 691–703.

Be60 Desonay, Fernand, 'Les Manifestes littéraires du XVIᵉ siècle en France', *BHR*, XIV (1952), 250–65.
.1 England, S. L., *YWMLS*, XIV (1952), 44.

Be61 . . . , 'Sur les origines de la satire anti-bourgeoise en France: un problème de méthode', *Le Flambeau* (Mar.–Apr. 1969), 141–63.* Review article of Bd2.

Be62 Drost, Wolfgang, 'Petrarchismo e realismo nella poesia di d'Aubigné giovane', *Rivista di letterature moderne e comparate*, XV (1962), 165–87.

Be63 Ducros, Franc, 'Au sujet de la rhétorique', *RLR*, LXXIX (1970), 51–78.
.1 Sharratt, P., *YWMLS*, XXXII (1970), 45–6.

Be64 Dullaert, Maurice, 'Un ami gantois de la Pléiade (Charles Utenhove)', *Le Cahier des Arts* (July 1959).*

Be65 Dunlop, Geoffrey A., 'The Sources of the Idyls of Jean Vauquelin de la Fresnaye', *MP*, XII (1914–5), 133–64.

Be66 Eckhoff, Lorentz, 'Aestetiske Vaerdier i det XVI aarhundredes Franska literatur', *Edda*, XI (1924), 181–97.*

Be67 Espiner-Scott, Janet G., 'The Sources of Spenser's *Amoretti*', *MLR*, XXII (1927), 189–95.

Be68 . . . , 'The Influence of Ronsard', *MLR*, XXII (1927), 446.

Be69 Façon, Nina, 'Umanism, iluminism și romantism in Italia și Franța', *Revista de Filologie Romanică și Germanică* (Bucarest), I (1957), 37–63.* ("Humanisme, époque des lumières, et Romantisme en Italie et en France").

Be70 ..., 'La Culture italienne et ses problèmes dans la pensée des écrivains depuis la Renaissance jusqu'à nos temps', *BRP,* VI (1967), 213–25.

Be71 Faguet, Emile, 'Evolution littéraire des hommes de la Pléiade', *RCC,* XXV, 1 (1923–4), 289–305, 385–403. (Index gives *Evolution,* title of article is *Education*).

Be72 Fletcher, Jefferson B., 'Spenser and the "Theatre of Worldlings" ', *MLN,* XIII (1898), 409–15.

Be73 ..., 'Areopagus and Pléiade', *Journal of English and Germanic Philology,* II (1898–9), 429–53.

Be74 Franchet, Henri, 'Erasme et Ronsard: la lettre *Contra quosdam* et le *Discours des misères de ce temps*', *RHLF,* XXXIX (1932), 321–38.

Be75 François, Alexis, 'D'une préfiguration de la langue classique au XVIe siècle', in *Mélanges... Abel Lefranc,* Paris: Droz, 1936, pp. 91–100.

Be76 Françon, Marcel, 'Notes sur le XVIe siècle français', *FR,* XXII (1948–9), 128–35.

Be77 ..., 'Note sur l'influence italienne en France au XVIe siècle', *Italica,* XXXII (1955), 115–9. Also in *Revue de l'Université d'Ottawa* (July–Sept. 1967).*

Be78 ..., 'La Question de la langue en France au XVIe siècle', *St. fr.,* II (1957), 257–9.

Be79 ..., 'Vérité et littérature: le thème du poète malade', *St. fr.,* V (1958), 243–6.

Be80 ..., 'Les Variantes du Mémoire de Nerval sur les poètes du XVIe siècle', *MLN,* LXXIV (1959), 711–3.

Be81 ..., 'Gérard de Nerval et les citations qu'il a faites dans son étude sur les poètes du XVIe siècle', *RBPH,* XXXVII (1959), 703–6.

Be82 ..., 'Le "monstre ignorance" au XVIe siècle', *St. fr.,* X (1960), 71–4.

Be83 ..., 'Note sur l'étude de Gérard de Nerval "Les poètes du XVIe siècle" ', *St. fr.,* XI (1960), 276–8.

Be84 . . . , 'L'Etude de Gérard de Nerval sur les poètes du XVIe siècle', *St. fr.*, XV (1961), 463–73. Reproduction of text published in *l'Artiste*, VIII (15.7.1852), 181–4; IX (1.8. 1852), 5–6; IX (15.8.1852), 22–4. See Be189.

Be85 . . . , 'L'Eloge de l'Italie et l'éloge de la France', *St. fr.*, XXIV (1964), 470–1.

Be86 . . . , 'Annibal Caro et la Pléiade', *Bulletin folklorique d'Ile-de-France* (Spring 1966).*

Be87 . . . , 'Sur "les belles matineuses" ', *Bulletin folklorique d'Ile-de-France* (Aut. 1967).*

Be88 . . . , 'Les Belles matineuses', *Romance Notes*, VIII (1966–7), 285–6.

Be89 . . . , 'Note sur Claudien et la Pléiade', *St. fr.*, XXXIII (1967), 476–8.

Be90 . . . , 'Deux notes d'un seiziémiste. (i) Sur le journal de Montaigne, (ii) Lyrisme et technique poétique', *FS,* XXII (1968), 99–106.
.1 Jeanneret, M., *St. fr.*, XXXVII (1969), 128.

Be91 . . . , 'Notes sur la littérature et l'histoire françaises du XVIe siècle. (IV, The Greek Anthology and "les belles matineuses")', *Quaderni francesi*, I (1970), 171–211.

Be92 Frank, Félix, 'Un Semblançay écrivain: la lettre de Jacques de Beaune en faveur de la langue française, éclaircissements et rectifications', *RHLF,* II (1895), 598–603. Reply to Bb218.

Be93 Frautschi, R. L., 'An example of the preposition "dans" in 1516', *Romance Notes,*I, (1960–1), 155–6.
.1 Sozzi, L., *St. fr.*, XV (1961), 532.

Be94 Fucilla, Joseph G., 'A Rhetorical Pattern in Renaissance and Baroque Poetry', *St. Ren.*, III (1956), 23–48.

Be95 Galland, René, 'Un poète errant de la Renaissance: Jean Van der Noot et l'Angleterre', *RLC,* II (1922), 337–50.

Be96 Galletier, Ed., 'L'*Idylle du Loir* du poète angevin Pierre Le Loyer, et ses sources antiques', *RSS,* V (1917), 147–61.

Be97 Gebelin, François, 'Un manifeste de l'école néo-classique en 1549: l'entrée de Henri II à Paris', *Bulletin de la Société d'histoire de Paris,* LX (1924), 35–45.

Be98 Gerig, John, 'Barthélemy Aneau', *RR,* XI, 10e année (1910), 182–97; XII, 11e année (1911), 1–17, 80–93.

Be99   Glatigny, Michel, 'Le Champ sémantique des parties du corps dans la poésie amoureuse de 1550', *FM*, XXXVII (1969), 7–34.
.1 Jeanneret, M., *St. fr.*, XXXIX (1969), 534.
.2 Wilson, D. B., *YWMLS*, XXX (1968), 74.

Be100   Godenne, R., 'Etienne Jodelle, traducteur de Virgile', *BHR*, XXXI (1969), 195–204.
.1 Jodogne, P., *St. fr.*, XXXIX (1969), 535.
.2 Wilson, D. B., *YWMLS*, XXXI (1969), 84.

Be101   Goldberg, Lea, 'Certain aspects of imitation and translation in poetry', in *Actes du IVe congrès de l'Association internationale de littérature comparée*, II, 1966, pp. 839–43.*

Be102   Gourg, J. L., 'L'Etude du XVIe siècle français en U.R.S.S.', *RLR*, LXXX (1972), 459–64.

Be103   Graham, Victor E., 'Some undiscovered sources of Desportes', *FS*, X (1956), 123–31.
.1 England, S. L. , *YWMLS*, XVIII (1956), 60.
.2 Nicholas, B. L., *St. fr.*, I (1957), 134.
.3 Rizza, C., *St. fr.*, I (1957), 136.

Be104   . . . , 'Music for Poetry in France', *Ren. News*, XVII (1964), 307–17.

Be105   Griffin, Robert, 'Jean de Sponde's "Sonnet de la Mort" XII: The World, the Flesh and the Devil', *Romance Notes*, IX (1967–8), 102–6.
.1 Richter, M., *St. fr.*, XXXVII (1969), 131–2.

Be106   Griffiths, Richard, 'Some Uses of Petrarchan Imagery in 16th-century French Poetry', *FS*, XVIII (1964), 311–21.
.1 Richter, M., *St. fr.*, XXVII (1965), 529.

Be107   Guy, Henri, 'Les Sources françaises de Ronsard', *RHLF*, VIII (1902), 217–56.

Be108   Hallowell, Robert E., 'Jean Le Blond's *défense* of the French language (1549)', *Rom. Rev.*, LI (1960), 86–92.
.1 Sozzi, L., *St. fr.*, XI (1960), 332.

Be109   . . . , 'Ronsard and the Gallic Hercules Myth', *St. Ren.*, IX (1962), 242–55.
.1 McFarlane, I. D., *YWMLS*, XXIV (1962), 81.
.2 Stefano, G. di, *St. fr.*, XXIII (1964), 334–5.

Be110   . . . , 'L'Hercule gallique: expression et image poétique', in Bd143, pp. 243–54.

Be111   Hardee, A. Maynor, 'Toward a Definition of the French Renaissance Novel', *St. Ren.*, XV (1968), 25–38.
.1 Jeanneret, M., *St. fr.*, XLI (1970), 329–30.

Be112   Harmer, L. C., 'Lancelot de Carle', *HR*, VI (1939), 443–74.

Be113   Harvitt, Hélène J., 'Hugues Salel, Poet and Translator', *MP*, XVI (1918–9), 595–605.

Be114   Hatzfeld, Helmut A., 'The Role of Mythology in Poetry during the French Renaissance', *MLQ*, XIII (1952), 392–404.

Be115   Hughes, Merritt Y., 'Spenser and the Greek Pastoral Triad', *SP*, XX, (1923), 184–215.

Be116   Hulubei, Alice, 'Virgile en France au XVIe siècle', *RSS*, XVIII (1931), 1–77.
.1 Tanquerey, F. J., *YWMLS*, III (1933), 47.

Be117   Hutton, James, 'The Classics in Sixteenth-Century France', *Classical Weekly*, XLIII, 9 (30.1.50), 131–8.

Be118   ... , 'The "lost" *Cohortatio pacificatoria* of Jacques Peletier du Mans', *BHR*, XXII (1960), 302–19.
.1 Sozzi, L., *St. fr.*, XII (1960), 534–5.

Be119   Jack, Ronald D. S., 'James VI and Renaissance Poetic Theory', *English*, XVI (Aut. 1967), 208–11.*

Be120   ... , 'Imitation in the Scottish Sonnet', *Comp. Lit.*, XX (1968), 313–28.
.1 Campagnoli, R., *St. fr.*, XLI (1970), 330.
.2 Wilson, D. B., *YWMLS*, XXX (1968), 75.

Be121   ... , 'The Poetry of Alexander Craig: A Study in imitation and originality', *FMLS*, V, (1969), 377–84.

Be122   Joukovsky, Françoise, 'Tombeaux et offrandes rustiques chez les poètes français et néo-latins du XVIe siècle', *BHR*, XXVII (1965), 226–47.
.1 McFarlane, I. D., *YWMLS*, XXVII (1965), 60.

Be123   ... , 'La Guerre des dieux et des géants chez les poètes français du XVIe siècle (1500–85)', *BHR*, XXIX (1967), 55–92.
.1 Jodogne, P., *St. fr.*, XXXV (1968), 337.
.2 Wilson, D. B., *YWMLS*, XXIX (1967), 43.

Be124   ... , 'Voyageurs français dans la Venise du XVIe siècle', *RLC*, XLI (1967), 481–507.
.1 Jodogne, P., *St. fr.*, XXXVIII (1969), 331.
.2 Wilson, D. B. , *YWMLS*, XXX (1968), 66.

Be125 . . . , 'L'Epicurisme poétique au XVIe siècle', in *Ass. G. Budé,* Congrès de Paris, Paris: Les Belles Lettres, 1969, pp. 639–75.

Be126 Jourda, Pierre, 'Glanes ronsardiennes. Augé Gaillard et la Pléiade', *RHLF,* XXXVI (1929), 223–30.

Be127 . . . , 'La Pléiade et les poètes antiques', in *Ass. G. Budé,* Congrès de Lyon (8–13 Sept. 1958), Paris: Les Belles Lettres, 1960, pp. 378–408.

Be128 Kastner, Léon E., 'L'Alternance des rimes depuis Octavien de Saint-Gelais jusqu'à Ronsard', *RLR,* XLVII (1904), 336–47.

Be129 . . . , 'The Scottish Sonneteers and the French Poets', *MLR,* III (1907–8), 1–15.

Be130 . . . , 'The Elizabethan Sonneteers and the French Poets', *MLR,* III (1907–8), 268–77.

Be131 . . . , 'Drummond of Hawthornden and the poets of the Pléiade', *MLR,* IV (1908–9), 329–41.

Be132 . . . , 'Spenser's *Amoretti* and Desportes', *MLR,* IV (1908–9), 65–9.

Be133 . . . , 'The Sources of Olivier de Magny's Sonnets', *MP,* VII (1909–10), 27–48.

Be134 Keller, Abraham C., 'Anti-War Writing in France 1500–1560', *PMLA,* LXVII (1952), 240–50.

Be135 Kelly, L. G., 'L'Enseignement du style littéraire pendant la Renaissance', *Revue de l'Université d'Ottawa* (July–Sept. 1967).*

Be136 Kerr, William A. R., 'The Pléiade and Platonism', *MP,* V (1907–8), 407–21.

Be137 Kibédi Varga, A., 'Poésie et Cosmologie au XVIe siècle', in Bd143, pp. 135–55.

Be138 Krüger, Paul, 'Omkring Plejaden', in *Fransk literaer Kritik indtil 1830,* Doctoral thesis, Copenhagen, 1936.*

Be139 Laumonier, Paul, 'L'*Art poétique* de Jacques Peletier du Mans', *RR,* I, 2e année (Jan.–June 1901), 248–76.

Be140 . . . , 'Luigi Alamanni, son influence sur la Pléiade', *RR,* IV, 3e année (June–Sept. 1903), 258–74. Review article of Bd101.

Be141 . . . , 'Ronsard pétrarquiste avant 1550', in *Mélanges . . . Gustave Lanson,* Paris: Hachette, 1922, pp. 109–14.

Be142   . . . , 'Une lettre de Peletier à Ronsard', in *Mélanges* . . .
Edmond Huguet, Paris: Boivin, 1940, pp. 177–83.

Be143   Laurens, P., Imitations de Properce en France au XVIe
siècle', *Orpheus* IX, (1962), 85–104.

Be144   Leake, R. E., 'Antoine Fouquelin and the Pléiade', *BHR,*
XXXII (1970), 379–94.
.1 Jodogne, P., *St. fr.,* XLIV (1971), 336.
.2 Sharratt, P., *YWMLS,* XXXII (1970), 86–7.

Be145   Lebègue, Raymond, 'Horace en France pendant la
Renaissance', *BHR,* III (1936), 141–64, 289–308, 384–
419.

Be146   . . . , 'Les Traductions en France pendant la Renaissance',
in *Ass. G. Budé,* Congrès de Strasbourg, 1938, Paris: Les
Belles Lettres, 1939, pp. 362–77.

Be147   . . . , 'L'Evolution de la forme poétique en France à la
fin de la Renaissance', *Comptes-rendus de l'Académie des
Inscriptions et Belles-Lettres* (1944), 397–405.*

Be148   . . . , 'Reports concerning French Literary and Linguistic
Studies in the Period 1940–1945: Renaissance and
Seventeenth Century', *MLR,* XLI (1946), 280–91.

Be149   . . . , 'La Langue des traducteurs français au XVIe siècle',
in *Festgabe Ernst Gamillscheg,* Tübingen, 1952, pp. 24–
30, Appendix, 31–4.

Be150   . . . , 'La Traduction et l'imitation dans la littérature
française du XVIe siècle', *L'Année propédeutique,* 5–6
(1952); XI, 1–2 (Nov. 1958), 20–7.*

Be151   . . . , 'Le Platonisme en France au XVIe siècle', in *Ass. G.
Budé,* Congrès de Tours et Poitiers, Paris: Les Belles Lettres,
1954, pp. 331–51.

Be152   . . . , 'La Pléiade et les beaux-arts', in *Atti del Quinto
Congresso Internazionale di Lingue e Letterature moderne,*
Florence, 1955, pp. 115–24.*

Be153   . . . , 'Les Confidences de Marguerite de Navarre', in
Festgabe für Fritz Neubert (Formen der Selbstdarstellung.
Analekten zu einer Geschichte des literarischen Selbst-
portraits), Berlin: Duncker & Humbolt, 1956, pp. 225–8.
.1 Neuhofer, P., *St. fr.,* XI (1960), 330.

Be154   . . . , 'Les Poètes antiques en France au XVIe siècle', in
Ass. G. Budé, Congrès de Lyon (8–13 Sept. 1958), Paris:
Les Belles Lettres, 1960, pp. 353–70.

Be155 . . . , 'La Première édition des *OEuvres* de Ronsard', *AUP* (1961), 54–7.*
.1 Sozzi, L., *St. fr.,* XVI (1962), 134–5.

Be156 . . . , 'De la Brigade à la Pléiade', in Bd143, pp. 13–20.

Be157 Leiner, Wolfgang, 'Von der Ruinenpoesie des 16. Jahrhunderts zur Schloss- und Parkpoesie des 17. Jahrhunderts. (Zu einem Sonett Castigliones und einem Sonett Malherbes)', *Germanisch-Romanische Monatsschrift,* XLVII (1966), 15–43.

Be158 Lorian, A., 'Les Latinismes de syntaxe en français', *ZFSL,* LXXVII (1967), 155–69.

Be159 Lote, Georges, 'L'Harmonie du vers français aux XVIe et XVIIe siècles', *Annales de la faculté des lettres d'Aix-en-Provence,* XXIII (1944).*

Be160 Lytton Sells, A., 'The Pléiade', in *Animal Poetry in French and English Literature and the Greek Tradition,* Indiana Univ. Publications (Humanities Series XXXV), 1955, pp. 56–75.

Be161 Mahieu, Robert G., 'L'Elégie au XVIe siècle. Essai sur l'histoire du genre', *RHLF,* XLVI (1939), 145–79.

Be162 Malden, Paul de, 'Les Pléiades', *BBB* (1846), 1117–34.*

Be163 Margolin, J. C., 'Le Roy, traducteur de Platon et la Pléiade', in Bd143, pp. 49–62.

Be164 Martin, H. J., 'Ce qu'on lisait à Paris au XVIe siècle', *BHR,* XXI (1959), 222–30.

Be165 Martinon, Philippe, 'Etude sur le vers français. La genèse des règles, de Jean Lemaire à Malherbe', *RHLF,* XVI (1909), 62–87.

Be166 Marty-Laveaux, Charles, 'La Langue de la Pléiade' in *Etudes de langue française,* Paris: A. Lemerre, 1901, pp. 69–114. See also Bd146.

Be167 Mayer, C. A., 'Coq-à-l'âne. Definition - Invention - Attributions', *FS,* XVI (1962), 1–11.
.1 McFarlane, I. D., *YWMLS,* XXIV (1962), 80.
.2 Sozzi, L., *St. fr.,* XVII (1962), 332.

Be168 McDiarmid, M. P., 'Notes on the poems of John Stewart of Baldynneis', *Review of English Studies,* XXIV (1948), 12–18.

Be169 McFarlane, Ian D., 'Jean Salmon Macrin (1490–1557)', *BHR,* XXI (1959), 55–84, 311–49; XXII (1960), 73–89.

Be170 ..., 'George Buchanan and France', in *Studies in French Literature presented to Harold W. Lawton,* Manchester UP, 1968, pp. 223–46.
.1 England, S. L., *MLR,* LXIV (1969), 663–4.
.2 Richter, M., *St. fr.,* XLII (1970), 531–2.
.3 Ullman, S., *FS,* XXIII (1969), 325–7.
.4 Wilson, D. B., *YWMLS,* XXX (1968), 64.

Be171 ..., 'George Buchanan's Latin Poems from Script to Print. A Preliminary Survey', *The Library,* 5th series, XXIV, 4 (Dec. 1969), 277–332.
.1 Wilson, D. B., *YWMLS,* XXXI (1969), 73.

Be172 ..., 'George Buchanan and French Humanism', in *Humanism in France at the End of the Middle Ages and in the Early Renaissance,* ed. A. H. T. Levi, Manchester UP, 1970, pp. 295–319.
.1 Sharratt, P., *YWMLS,* XXXII (1970), 78.

Be173 McPeek, James A. S., 'Major Sources of Spenser's *Epithalamion',Journal of English and Germanic Philology,* XXXV (1936), 183–213.

Be174 Merrill, Robert V., 'Platonism in Pontus de Tyard's *Erreurs amoureuses* (1549)', *MP,* XXXV (1937–8), 139–58.

Be175 ..., 'Ronsard and the Burning Grove', *MP,* XXXVII (1939–40), 337–41.

Be176 ..., 'Eros and Anteros', *Speculum,* XIX (1944), 265–84.

Be177 ..., 'The Pléiade and the Androgyne', *Comp. Lit.,* I, (1949), 97–112.

Be178 Michajlov, A. D., 'Quelques traits de la Renaissance française', in *Literatura epochi Vozroždenija i problemy vsemirnoj literatury,* Moscow: Izdatelstvo "Nauka", 1967, pp. 284–314.*
.1 Soloviev, A. V., *BHR,* XXX (1968), 442–3.

Be179 Michajlowska, Teresa, 'Genological notions in the Renaissance theory of poetry', *Zagadnienia rodzajów literackich,* XII, 2 (23), (1970), 5–20.*

Be180 Michaut, Gustave, 'Le Tableau de la poésie française au XVIe siècle', in *Etudes sur Sainte-Beuve,* Paris: Fontemoing, 1905, pp. 141–232.

Be181 Michel, Pierre, 'La Chatte de Montaigne parmi les chats du XVIe siècle', *Bulletin de la Société des Amis de Montaigne,* XXIX (1964), 14–18.

Be182 Minguzzi, A., 'L'Ecole romantique et la Pléiade', *Culture française* (Bari), VIII (1961), 199–204.*

Be183 Morel-Fatio, Alfred, 'Histoire d'un sonnet', *RHLF,* I (1894), 97–102. See Bb82.

Be184 Morrison, Mary, 'Three versions of an elegy of Catullus: an undetected source of Desportes', *FS,* XIII (1959), 1-10.
.1 McFarlane, I. D., *YWMLS,* XXI (1959), 61.
.2 Sozzi, L., *St. fr.,* VIII (1959), 302–3.

Be185 . . . , 'Catullus and the poetry of the Renaissance in France. I Baïf and Catullus, II Du B. and Catullus', *BHR,* XXV (1963), 25–56.
.1 McFarlane, I. D., *YWMLS,* XXV (1963), 44.
.2 Mombello, G., *St. fr.,* XXI (1963), 537.

Be186 Müller, Armand, 'Les Ecrivains du XVIe siècle et la Réforme', *L'Ecole* (21.9.63), 2, 67–8.*
.1 Richter, M., *St. fr.,* XXV (1965), 136.

Be187 Musso, G. G.,'La cultura genovese fra il Quattro e il Cinquecento', *Miscellenea di Storia Ligure* (Univ. di Genova), I (1958), 123–87.*
.1 Sozzi, L., *St. fr.,* X (1960), 129.

Be188 Nerval, Gérard de, 'De l'école de Ronsard au XVIe siècle', *Mercure de France au XIXe siècle,* XXXIV (1831), 385–96.

Be189 . . . , 'Les Poètes du XVIe siècle', *L'Artiste,* VIII (15.7. 1852), 181–4; IX (1.8.1852), 5–6, (15.8.1852), 22–4.* See Be84.

Be190 Neubert, Fritz, 'Einführung in die französische und italienische Epistolarliteratur der Renaissance und ihre Probleme', *Rom. Jahrb.,* XII (1961), 67–93.
.1 Drost, W., *St. fr.,* XX (1963), 333.

Be191 Nolhac, Pierre de, 'Un humaniste ami de Ronsard: Pierre de Paschal, historiographe de la France', *RHLF,* XXV (1918), 32–59, 243–61, 362–87.

Be192 . . . , 'Quelques provinciaux amis de la Pléiade', *Revue des études historiques* (1921), 28–36.*

Be193 . . . , 'La Pléiade et le latin de la Renaissance', *RF,* 1re année, no. 7 (15.6.21), 742–54.

Be194 Noyer-Weidner, Alfred, 'Ronsards Antike-Nachahmungen und die mittelalterlich-französische Tradition', in *Festschrift für Gerhard Rohlfs,* Halle, 1958, pp. 319–35.
.1 Barnbeck, M., *St. fr.,* XI (1960), 333.

Be195   Pergameni, H., 'La Satire du XVIe siècle et les *Tragiques* d'Agrippa d'Aubigné', *Revue de Belgique,* XXXIX (1881); XL (1882).*

Be196   Picot, Emile, 'Pour et contre l'influence italienne en France au XVIe siècle', *Etudes italiennes,* II (1920), 17–32.

Be197   Pienaar, W. L. B., 'Edmund Spenser and Junker J. vander Noot', *English Studies* (Apr. 1926), 33–44, 67–76.

Be198   Piquard, M., 'La Bibliothèque d'un homme d'état au XVIe siècle', in *Mélanges . . . Frantz Calot,* Paris, 1960, pp. 227–35.
    .1   Sozzi, L., *St. fr.,* XIV (1961), 329.

Be199   Piron, Maurice, ' "En forme de pasquils." Contribution à l'étude des genres littéraires au XVIe siècle', in *Mélanges . . . Pierre Jourda,* Paris: Nizet, 1970, pp. 131–56.

Be200   Plattard, Jean, 'Chroniques: Bulletin d'histoire littéraire', *RSS,* I (1913), 444–53.

Be201   . . . , 'Les Arts et les artistes de la Renaissance française jugés par les écrivains du temps', *RHLF,* XXI (1914), 481–502.

Be202   . . . , 'L'Université de Poitiers au temps de Ronsard', *RCC,* XXVI, 1 (28.2.25), 560–70.

Be203   . . . , 'Un novateur dans l'enseignement du droit romain. François de Nesmond. Professeur à l'Université de Poitiers (1555)', *RSS,* XII (1925), 141–7.

Be204   Plazolles, L. R., 'Signification et portée des réflexions doctrinales de la Pléiade', *L'Année propédeutique,* XI, 1–2 (Nov. 1958), 14–19.*

Be205   Plessy, Bernard, 'Roses pour l'hiver', *Le Bulletin des lettres* (15.2.69).*

Be206   Podgajeckaja, I. Ju., 'L'Art poétique de la Pléiade', in *Literatura epochi Vozroždenija i problemy vsemirnoj literatury,* Moscow: Izdatelstvo "Nauka", 1967, pp. 315–39.*
    .1   Soloviev, A. V., *BHR,* XXX (1968), 442–3.

Be207   Prescott, Anne L., 'The Reputation of Clément Marot in Renaissance England', *St. Ren.,* XVIII (1971), 173–202.

Be208   Prinsen, J., 'Jean Van Hout, l'initiateur de la Hollande aux principes de la Pléiade (1543–1609)', *RR,* VIII, 7e année (June–Oct. 1907), 121–35.

Be209   Quainton, Malcolm D., 'Ronsard's philosophic and cosmo-
         logical conceptions of time', *FS*, XXIII (1969), 1–22.
         .1 Jeanneret, M., *St. fr.*, XXXIX (1969), 535.
         .2 Wilson, D. B., *YWMLS*, XXXI (1969), 83.

Be210   Raymond, Marcel, 'Jean Tagaut. Poète français et
         bourgeois de Genève', *RSS*, XII (1925), 98–140.

Be211   . . . , 'Deux pamphlets inconnus contre Ronsard et la
         Pléiade', *RSS*, XIII (1926), 243–64.

Be212   . . . , 'La Pléiade et le Maniérisme', in Bd143, pp. 391–423.

Be213   Reboul, P., 'Sur trois vers de Sénèque au XVIe siècle', *RSH*,
         n.s. XLV (1947), 75–9.

Be214   Redman, Harry, 'New Thomas Sebillet Data', *St. fr.*,
         XXXVIII (1969), 201–9.

Be215   Renwick, W. L., 'The Critical Origins of Spenser's Diction',
         MLR, XVII (1922), 1–16.

Be216   . . . , 'Spenser and the Pléiade', *MLR*, XVII (1922), 287–8.

Be217   Révillout, Charles, 'Lettre d'Eustache Du Bellay au
         Cardinal Jean Du Bellay (28.12.1559)', *Mémoires lus à la
         Sorbonne* (1867).* See *RR*, IV (1903), 47.

Be218   Ridgely, B. S., 'The Cosmic Voyage in French Sixteenth-
         Century Learned Poetry', *St. Ren.*, X (1963), 136–62.

Be219   Rossettini-Trtnik, Olga, 'Les Poésies inconnues de
         Battista Alamanni, évêque de Mâcon, fils de Luigi
         Alamanni [et leurs relations avec celles de Du B]',
         Rivista di Letteratura Moderne e Comparate, XV (1962),
         54–65.
         .1 Mombello, G., *St. fr.*, XX (1963), 338–9.

Be220   Rouault, Joseph, 'Sous le signe de Coqueret – premiers
         documents originaux sur le Collège de Coqueret', *Eurydice*,
         cahier 4 (Oct. 1933), no pagination.*

Be221   Rousset, Jean, 'Les Recueils de sonnets sont-ils com-
         posés? ', in Bd93, pp. 203–15.

Be222   Sage, Pierre, 'Autour de l' "Hercule Chrestien" ', *Bulletin
         des Facultés Catholiques de Lyon* (Jul.–Dec. 1960), 5–
         17.* Résumé under title 'L'Hercule Chrétien', in *Ass. G.
         Budé*, Congrès de Lyon (8–13 Sept. 1958), Paris: Les
         Belles Lettres, 1960, pp. 442–4.
         .1 Sozzi, L., *St. fr.*, XVII (1962), 334–5.

Be223   Satterthwaite, Alfred W., 'A reexamination of Spenser's translations of the "Sonets" from *A Theatre for Worldlings'*, *Philological Quarterly*, XXXVIII (1959), 509–15.

Be224   Saulnier, V. L., 'Autour de Maurice Scève: deux aspects internationaux de la Renaissance lyonnaise', *AUP*, XVIII (1948), 151–8.*

Be225   . . . , 'Les Poètes de la prise de Calais (1558)', *BBB*, n.s. (1949), 270–4.

Be226   . . . , 'Sur Jean Pellisson et quelques-uns de ses amis', *BHR*, XVII (1955), 80–6.

Be227   . . . , 'Malherbe et le XVIe siècle', *Bulletin de la Société d'Etude du XVIIe siècle*, XXXI (Apr. 1956), 195–229.*

Be228   . . . , 'Hommes pétrifiés et pierres vives. (Autour d'une formule de Panurge)', *BHR*, XXII (1960), 393–402.
         .1 Sozzi, L., *St. fr.*, XII (1960), 530.

Be229   Schaettel, Maurice, 'Rhétorique et Eurythmie dans une suite de quatrains de Ronsard', *CAIEF*, XXII (1970), 25–40.

Be230   Schmidt, Albert-Marie, 'Poètes lyonnais du seizième siècle', *Information littéraire*, 4e année, 3 (May–June 1952), 90–5; 4 (Sept.–Oct. 1952), 127–31.

Be231   Schneegans, F. Ed., 'A propos d'une note sur une fresque mythologique du XVIe siècle', *HR*, II (1935), 441–4.

Be232   Schunk, Peter, 'Um den zeitlichen Vorrang bei der Gattungsnachahmung. Zum Werk von Jean Vauquelin de la Fresnaie', *ZFSL*, LXXIX (1969), 207–23.
         .1 Dierlamm, W., *St. fr.*, XLV (1971), 532–3.

Be233   Séché, Léon, 'Le "Ronsard" de Victor Hugo', *Mercure de France*, XCV (Jan. 1912), 295–311.

Be234   Shorey, Paul, 'Le "Double Mont" in French Renaissance Poetry', *MP*, XIX (1921–2), 221–2.

Be235   Silver, Isidore, 'Ronsard's Ethical Thought', *BHR*, XXIV (1962), 88–117, 339–74.

Be236   . . . , 'Ronsard's Reflections on Cosmogony and Nature', *PMLA*, LXXIX (1964), 219–33.
         .1 McFarlane, I. D., *YWMLS*, XXVI (1964), 67.

Be237   . . . , 'The Formative Influences in Ronsard's Poetry', *SP*, LXIII (1966), 630–60.
         .1 McFarlane, I. D., *YWMLS*, XXVIII (1966), 66.

Be238   ..., 'The Theological Reaction, and the Creation of a National Poetic Language', *EC,* X (1970), 95–103.
.1 Sharratt, P., *YWMLS,* XXXII (1970), 85.

Be239   Simone, Franco, 'Quattro lettere di Jacques Peletier du Mans', *Rivista di Letterature Moderne e Comparate,* I (1946), 173–88.

Be240   ..., 'La Coscienza della Rinascita negli umanisti francesi', *Rivista di Letterature Moderne e Comparate,* I (1946), 249–76; II (1947), 11–33, 218–36.

Be241   ..., 'I poeti della Pléiade ed i loro predecessori', *Giornale italiano di Filologia,* II (1949), 229–37.

Be242   ..., 'Ronsard et l'histoire littéraire de son temps', *CAIEF,* XXII (1970), 53–72.

Be243   Spear, Frederick A., 'An Inquiry concerning Ronsard and the Sonnet Form', *MLN,* LXXIV (1959), 709–11.
.1 Sozzi, L., *St. fr.,* XIII (1961), 140.

Be244   Stackelberg, Jürgen von, 'Renaissance Wiedergeburt oder Wiederwuchs? ', *BHR,* XXII (1960), 406–20.
.1 Mölk, U., *St. fr.,* XVII (1962), 329.

Be245   ..., 'Ronsard und Aristoteles', *BHR,* XXV (1963), 349–61.

Be246   ..., 'Übersetzung und Imitatio in der französischen Renaissance', *Arcadia,* I (1966), 167–73.
.1 Dierlamm, W., *St. fr.,* XL (1970), 135.

Be247   Starobinski, Jean,'L'Encre de la mélancolie', *NRF,* XXI (1963), 410–23.

Be248   Stevens, Linton C., 'The Reputation of Lucian in 16th-Century France', *St. fr.,* XXXIII (1967), 401–6.

Be249   Sutherland, G. M., 'Proper names in Renaissance poetry', in Bd93, pp. 267–86.

Be250   Thibault, G., 'Anthoine de Bertrand, musicien de Ronsard et ses amis toulousains', in *Mélanges . . . Abel Lefranc,* Paris: Droz, 1936, pp. 282–300. See Bb17, Bd17.

Be251   Tilley, Arthur, 'The Composition of the Pléiade', *MLR,* VI (1911), 212–5.

Be252   ..., 'From Marot to Ronsard', in *Mélanges . . . Paul Laumonier,* Paris: Droz, 1935, pp. 131–61.

Be253   Toldo, P., 'Etudes sur la poésie burlesque française de la Renaissance', *ZRP,* XXV (1901), 71–93, 215–29, 257–77, 385–410, 513–32.

Be254 Trousson, Raymond, 'Le Mythe de Prométhée et de Pandore chez Ronsard', *BGB* (1961), 351–9.

Be255 Vaganay, Hugues, 'A propos de Ronsard', *RSS*, VI (1918), 114–6.

Be256 . . . , 'Une strophe lyrique au XVIe siècle', in *Mélanges . . . Joseph Vianey*, Paris: Les Presses Françaises, 1934, pp. 175–86.

Be257 . . . , 'Quatre noms propres dans la littérature: Délie, Philothée, Ophélie, Pasithée', *RLC*, XV (1935), 279–88.

Be258 Vianey, Joseph, 'L'Arioste et la Pléiade', *Bull. it.*, I, (1901), 295–317.

Be259 . . . , 'Les Origines du sonnet régulier', *RR*, IV, 3e année (Feb.–Mar. 1903), 74–93.

Be260 . . . , 'La Nature dans la poésie française au XVIe siècle', in *Mélanges . . . Paul Laumonier*, Paris: Droz, 1935, pp. 171–88.

Be261 Vipper, Ju. B., 'Les Traditions de la Renaissance et les voies de développement de la poésie et du drame en France au début du XVIIe siècle', in *Literatura epochi Vozrož-denija i problemy vsemirnoj literatury*, Moscow: Izdatelstvo "Nauka", 1967, pp. 340–81.*
.1 Soloviev, A. V., *BHR*, XXX (1968), 442–3.

Be262 Wardropper, Bruce W., 'The poetry of ruins in the Golden Age', *Revista hispánica moderna*, XXXV (1969), 295–305.

Be263 Warshaw, J., 'Recurrent préciosité', *MLN*, XXXI (1916), 129–35.

Be264 Weber, Henri, 'Poésie polémique et satirique de la Réforme sous les règnes de Henri II, François II et Charles IX', *CAIEF*, X (1958), 89–118.

Be265 . . . , 'Les Corrections de Ronsard dans les *Amours* de 1552', in *Studi in onore di V. Lugli e D. Valeri*, II, Venice: Neri-Pozza, 1961, pp. 989–1015.
.1 Sozzi, L., *St. fr.*, XVI (1962), 134.

Be266 . . . , 'Platonisme et sensualité dans la poésie amoureuse de la Pléiade', in Bd143, pp. 157–94.

Be267 . . . , 'Structure des odes chez Ronsard', *CAIEF*, XXII (1970), 99–118.

Be268 Weinberg, Bernard, 'The Problem of Literary Aesthetics in Italy and France in the Renaissance', *MLQ*, XIV (1953), 448–56.

Du Bellay: a bibliography

Be269   ..., 'L'Imitation au XVIe et au XVIIe siècles', *Proceedings of the IVth Congress of the International Comparative Literature Association,* Fribourg (1964), The Hague, 1966, pp. 697–703.*
.1 McFarlane, I. D., *YWMLS,* XXVIII (1966), 59.

Be270   Weise, Georg, 'Manierismo e Letteratura', *Rivista di Letterature Moderne e Comparate,* XIII, (1960), 5–52.
.1 Morabito, P., *St. fr.,* XX (1963), 332–3.

Be271   Wenderoth, Georg, 'Die poetischen Theorien des französischen Plejade in M. Opitz' deutscher Poeterei', *Euphorion,* XIII (1906), 445–68.

Be272   Wiley, William L., 'The French Renaissance gallicized: an emphasis on national tradition', *SP,* XXXIV (1937), 248–59.

Be273   Will, Sam F., 'Camille de Morel; a prodigy of the Renaissance', *PMLA,* LI (1930), 83–119.
.1 Lawton, H. W., *YWMLS,* VII (1937), 47.

Be274   Williams, R. C., 'Metrical form of the epic, as discussed by 16th-century critics', *MLN,* XXXVI (1921), 449–57.

Be275   Wilson, Dudley B., 'Le Blason', in Bd143, pp. 97–112.

Be276   Wilson, Harold S., 'Some Meanings of Nature in Renaissance Literary Theory', *Journal of the History of Ideas,* II, 4 (Oct. 1941), 430–48.

Be277   Wyndham, George, 'The Pléiade', *Cosmpolis,* II (1897), 24–48.*

INDEX OF NAMES

* * *

Ackermann, Paul, Ab1
Adamany, Richard G., Bc1
Addamanio, Natale, Ba1; Bb1; Bd1
Adler, Alfred, Bb2
Aebly, Hedwig, Ba2
Alamanni, Battista, Be219
Alamanni, Luigi, Bd101; Be140, 219
Allem, Maurice, Bb3
Alter, Jean V., Bd2
Amato, Modesto, Ba3
Ambrière, Francis, Ba4; Bb4
Amsler, Roger, Bb5
Amyot, Jacques, Bd21; Be6
Ancenis, Catherine d', Bb259
Andrieux, Maurice, Bb6
Aneau, Barthélemy (Quintil Horatien, q.v.), Be98
Anon., Ab6.1; Ba15.1, 15a.l; Bb7, 8, 9; Bd34.1, 71.1, 92.1; Be1, 2
Annius of Vitebo, Bc2
Antonioli, R., Ba52.1
Apollo, Bc55; Bd144
Arens, John C., Bb10
Areopagus, Be73
Aretino, Pietro, Bc78
Ariosto, Ludovico, Bd30, 39, 212; Be258
Aristotle, Be245
Armstrong, Elizabeth, Bd3, 31.1, 49.1, 80.1, 175.1
Arnold, Ivor D.O., Be3
Arthos, J., Ba58.1
Asher, R. E., Bc2
Atkins, J. W. H., Bd9.1, 96.1
Atkinson, James B., Bc3
Aubert de Poitiers, Guillaume, Ba5
Aubertin, Charles, Bd5
Aubigné, Agrippa d', Bc11, 14, 19, 49; Bd8, 117, 232; Be62, 195
Augé-Chiquet, Mathieu, Bd6
Aulotte, Robert, Bd203.1; Be4, 5, 6
Ausonius, Bb193
Azibert, Mireille M. L., Bc4

Babelon, Jean, Bd7
Baïf, Jean-Antoine de, Bb141, 173; Bc83; Bd6; Be185
Bailbé, Jacques, Bd8, 122.1, 206.1, 238.1; Be7, 8
Baillet, Adrien, Bb11; Bd149
Baillou, Jean, Bd88.1; Be9
Baldwin, Charles S., Bd9
Ballu, Camille, Bb24
Balmas, Enea, Bd10, 93.1; Be10
Banašević, Nicolas, Bd11
Bannerman, Edith I., Bc5
Banta, Josephine D., Bc6
Barnbeck, M., Be194.1
Baron, Hans, Be11
Batault, Georges, Be12
Baudelaire, Charles, Bd68
Baumgartner, E., Bd187.1
Baur, Albert, Bd12
Bazin, René, Bb12
Beall, Chandler B., Bd39.1; Be13
Beaune, Jacques de, Be92
Beaupère, Thérèse, Ba6
Beauplan, Robert de, Ae2
Becker, Abraham H., Bd13
Becker, G., Ba60.1; Bd131.1
Becker, Karl, Bd14
Bellaud, Be28
Belleau, Rémy, Ba7; Bb100, 171, 173; Bd50, 60
Beller, M., Be13.1
Bellesort, André, Be14
Belleuvre, P., Bb13
Belloc, Hilaire, Bb14
Belowski, Eleonore, Bb15
Beltrand, Jacques, Ae3
Bémol, M., Bd156.1
Benesch, Otto, Be15
Bensimon, Marc, Bd203.2; Be16
Berdan, John, M., Be17
Berger, Bertrand, Bb239
Berger, Bruno, Bd15

101

INDEX OF WORKS

* * *